Thinking in Your Right Mind

Allow the Power of God to Change the Way You Think

Henry Thomas Hamblin

Hamblin Vision Publishing

Copyright

© Copyright 2025 Hamblin Vision Publishing - all rights reserved.

The content contained within this book may not be reproduced, duplicated or transmitted without direct written permission from the author or the publisher.

Under no circumstances will any blame or legal responsibility be held against the publisher, or author, for any damages, reparation, or monetary loss due to the information contained within this book, either directly or indirectly.

Legal Notice:

This book is copyright protected. It is only for personal use. You cannot amend, distribute, sell, use, quote or paraphrase any part, or the content within this book, without the consent of the author or publisher.

Disclaimer Notice:

Please note the information contained within this document is for educational and entertainment purposes only. All effort has been executed to present accurate, up to date, reliable, complete information. No warranties of any kind are declared or implied. Readers acknowledge that the author is not engaged in the rendering of legal, financial, medical or professional advice. The content within this book has been derived from various sources. Please consult a licensed professional before attempting any techniques outlined in this book.

By reading this document, the reader agrees that under no circumstances is the author responsible for any losses, direct or indirect, that are incurred as a result of the use of the information contained within this document, including, but not limited to, errors, omissions, or inaccuracies.

Contents

Introduction	VIII
Concise Biography of Henry Thomas Hamblin By John Delafield, Hamblin's grandson	XI
1. Transforming Thought Through the Power of the Infinite	1
2. Empowering Visualisations and Affirmations	10
3. Finding The Good in Life	19
4. Learning Through Non-Resistance From Letting Go	27
5. Harmony And Peace Through Love and Forgiveness	36
6. The Secret of Unity and Harmony	44
7. Faith	52
8. Overcoming Temptation	61
9. Overcoming Habit	69
10. Overcoming Adversity and Trouble	78

11.	Unity and Oneness Divine guidance and protection	87
12.	Divine Union	95

A Guide to Right Thinking in Action
Practical Applications and Examples of Right Thinking

13.	But what IS Right Thinking?	106
14.	The Effect Of Thought	115
15.	The Greatest Achievement	119
16.	Happiness	122
17.	Power	126
18.	True Prosperity	131
19.	Health and Healing	137
20.	Absolute Certainty	139
21.	Mastery Of Fate	142
22.	Self Confidence	145
23.	Peace	147
24.	Self Development	149
25.	Inspiration and Intuition	151
26.	Success and Achievement	153
27.	Good	155
28.	The Path of Attainment	157
29.	The Harmonious Life	160

30.	Divine Optimism	162
31.	The Greatest Of These Is Love	164
Also by Henry Thomas Hamblin		168

Introduction

HT Hamblin was a prolific author of a range of books, booklets and pamphlets offering practical advice on how to live in harmony with God, or what he sometimes referred to as *Source, the Universe,* or *the Cosmic.* However, this was not just a spiritual quest, or an attempt to avoid the troubles and cares of everyday life – far from it, for Hamblin was a very practical mystic – but a practical guide to each one to follow to increase health, happiness, and prosperity.

Hamblin founded the *Science of Thought Institute*, offering a course of practical lessons intended to guide his many thousands of students towards a happier, healthier and more prosperous life and, although he is sadly no longer with us in person, he left a wonderful legacy of publications that he had written from 1921 up to the time of his death in 1958. Some of those are still in print and available from **The Hamblin Trust** on www.thehamblinvision.org.uk but many have since gone out of print.

Conscious that the Trust will not be around forever, the custodians of Hamblin's teachings, the trustees of the Hamblin Trust, have decided to produce copies of Hamblin's earlier works in digital format to leave a legacy for future generations.

However, this is not one of Hamblin's earlier books. It is a series of 12 lessons that were discovered in the Trust's archives produced, at the time, under the heading of *'Science of Thought Course no. 3'*. The practical nature of the lessons contained in this book provide an essential guidance in what Hamblin described in the original lessons as *'Practical, Scientific, Controlled, Directed, and Elevated Thinking'*. It was felt that this new material very much complemented Hamblin's teachings in *'The Little Book of Right Thinking'* and we have therefore included both in one compilation.

Whilst the style of writing may now seem a little dated, Hamblin's teachings remain valid. We have therefore edited them a little to bring them more into line with current editorial style and, in recognition of Hamblin's regular references to 'the Mind of God', we have published this new compilation under the heading of *'Thinking in Your Right Mind'*.

The material in this compilation offers Hamblin's personal insights and practical guidance on transforming our lives, both spiritually and practically, leading to greater health, happiness, and joy. Although the 12 lessons start simply with practical techniques to apply to aid success in our everyday activities, they grow deeper as they progress to the more sublime heights of spiritual attainment. Lessons 6 – 12 have subject headings provided in the original documents, lessons 1-5 did not have these so we have added our own for consistency to indicate to the reader the nature of each lesson for ease of quick reference in need.

It is our hope that this compilation will, indeed, help *you* to achieve the health, success and happiness that the right application of Hamblin's teachings can provide and the sheer joy that arises from living in accordance with the spiritual insights he shares.

We wish you every blessing on your journey.

Noel Raine

Chair of the trustees
The Hamblin Trust

Concise Biography of Henry Thomas Hamblin

By John Delafield, Hamblin's
Grandson

Who was Henry Thomas Hamblin?

Henry Thomas Hamblin was a spiritual teacher and writer based in Sussex, England, whose message and vision were straightforward and pragmatic. He believed that the spiritual life and the practical, everyday life were inseparable. His teachings centred around the power of thought and the importance of meditation to draw on the inner power, wisdom and love that we all have deep within us. Hamblin referred to this as "the Secret Place of the Most High" in the days before meditation was widely practiced in the West.

Hamblin was colloquially known as HTH, and later 'The Saint of Sussex'. Whilst his teachings leaned towards esoteric Christianity, his philosophy was truly universal, embracing the truths of all faiths. The emphasis of his message is on finding the power of spirituality within us all, in the context of our everyday lives, rather than religion. As a young man, he reacted against the dogma of his strict, religious upbringing, and believed that religion often divided people, while spirituality united people. His teachings came from a place of pure empathy and compassion for humankind.

Henry Thomas Hamblin worked right up to the end of his life in 1958 and left a legacy that continues to this day, its voice as much needed now as it ever was.

A Wayward Child

Henry Thomas Hamblin was born in 1873 in Walworth, South East London, of Kentish parents, and was the second of two sons. His father was very religious, and his grandfather a minister of the Baptist Church. His mother, although of diminutive size, was reportedly "great of soul" and ruled the family with benevolent autocracy. The family was poor, very poor, like all those living around them in that district of London in the late Victorian era, and, despite their hard work, the only education that could be afforded for Henry was an elementary one. He followed this with a course in technology, which proved to be of inestimable value to a youth who was considered by his parents and teachers to be wayward.

"Unstable as water; thou shall not excel," his mother reproached him regularly. No doubt she intended it to shame her son into a regime of self-improvement, in keeping with child-rearing practices of the time, but it was hardly confidence-inspiring! "Slacker!" was the repeated insult from his elder brother. Wiser, more objective, heads might have paused for long enough to recognise a certain potential in the young boy who, at the age of nine, could attempt the writing of a school newspaper. He had also established himself as something of an elocutionist. Writing and speaking would both prove valuable skills in later life.

His adolescent years gave little indication of an error in the family verdict. "Henry the wayward" moved from one poorly paid post to another, idled in between dead-end jobs, succumbed to bouts of ill-health, and, before he had reached the age of eighteen, had displayed more than the usual "adolescent failings", according to his autobiography, *The Story of My Life*. From a modern perspective, all these Victorian euphemisms point to Hamblin being something of a "bad lad", an impression added to by his own heavy hints that he had been no stranger to drinking and carousing. He suffered terribly from pangs of regret following his periods of over-indulgence, so that "Henry the sinner" became "Henry the saint" – until the next time. His pronounced rebellious streak landed him in hot water more than once. He constantly pushed against the boundaries of the fire-and-brimstone brand of Christianity in which he had been raised, which he felt to be unbearably restrictive. Reading about his struggles with authority as a young man somehow makes the rather aloof spiritual writer he became more accessible and endearing; it's hard not to warm to someone who so openly confesses their own faults and shortcomings, especially in the tightly buttoned-up era in which he lived. He was inspired by books, many of which fired his worldly ambition and prompted his spiritual imagination.

What his parents and educators overlooked was that Hamblin was a young man with huge aspiration, flushed with a youthful zest for life, and inspired by a worthy ambition to rise above the rut of his circumstances. Although he pushed against his father's dogmatic and punitive style of practising religion, at heart, he was deeply religious. A person's early environment, education, and adolescent behaviour can often determine the course of their life. Youthful indulgences of one sort or another are inevitable. Hamblin's studies of the New Testament, which revealed that selfishness and hypocrisy, rather than indulgence, received greater condemnation by Jesus, would have been very much in his consciousness.

A Successful Businessman

There is no doubt that Hamblin had an enquiring mind, and this, coupled with a desire for scientific accuracy, enabled him to achieve success in his later endeavours in business. In this, despite his lack of education, he was bolstered by boundless faith and courage, which, coupled with a shrewd business sense, ensured that he succeeded beyond all expectation. In 1898, having taught himself opthalmics at night, he qualified as an optician and set up his first successful business as an optician, Theodore Hamblin (now Dolland and Aitchison), frequented by royalty, the rich and the famous.

Hamblin was a natural entrepreneur and a born risk-taker. By this time, he was also a family man. He married Eva Elizabeth in 1902, and they went on to have two sons and a daughter. He enjoyed acquiring several businesses, all with insufficient capital, and relying on credit and goodwill. He took more pleasure in the thrill of the challenge than in the promise of monetary gain. Far from being downcast in the face of numerous setbacks, he thrived on negotiating obstacles which appeared insurmountable. As soon as the business was established and running smoothly, however, rather than being satisfied with financial security and the ability to provide for his family, Hamblin's interest started to wane. He felt a loss of the initial drive and motivation, his physical and mental health began to decline... until the next big idea came along and away he would charge again, all fired up and raring to go.

Throughout all his wild days of youth and high-risk business ventures, Hamblin felt a great tug towards discovering a deeper meaning to life, beyond that of the daily struggle to make ends meet. Propelled by his discontent, he became a driven seeker after truth. In his quest, he met other prominent thinkers of the time and formed lasting friendships.

As his business success grew, so did a gnawing sense of depression. It was as if there was something inside him that had not yet found a voice. Around this time, he discovered the New Thought movement and began to read their publications. Hamblin realised then that none of his worldly success had made him happy. He felt that a move from London to the coast would be beneficial.

Shortly afterwards came the outbreak of the First World War, and Hamblin went off to serve his country, leaving his business in the care of others, almost with a sense of gleeful relief, strange though it sounds. But it was the sudden and unexpected death of his younger son at the age of ten, in 1918, that brought him to rock bottom and to question everything.

A Very Practical Mystic

Hamblin was not a genius, and millions of other people have made good in the world with even less promising assets. But it was in the second half of his life, when Hamblin turned away from creating highly successful business enterprises to focus instead on the spiritual realm, that his unique combination of the pragmatic and the profoundly spiritual shone forth. He has sometimes been described as a very practical mystic.

Hamblin began writing in the 1920s. The words seemed to flow from him. He found that writing clarified his thoughts. One of his first books written in this new phase of his career was *Within You Is The Power*, which was to sell over 200,000 copies. Other books soon followed. Hamblin believed that there is a source of abundance which, when contacted, could change a person's entire life. As long as people blamed their external circumstances for any misfortune, they were stuck in the 'victim role'; but if they moved in harmony with their inner source, their life could be full of abundance and harmony.

Soon after this, Hamblin set up a magazine called *The Science of Thought Review*, based on the principles of Applied Right Thinking. He wasn't discouraged by the fact that he had no experience of editing or publishing. His experience had taught him that if the mind worked in harmony with the Divine, then everything you needed flowed towards you. Anyone with any business sense at all knew that to set up a magazine with a first print run of 10,000 copies would be a risky thing to do. But Hamblin was not risk averse, to put it mildly! He wanted to put what he believed into practice. The only magazine of its kind in the 1920s, it soon gained a worldwide readership. Among his friends and contemporaries that were to contribute to the magazine were Joel Goldsmith, Henry Victor Morgan, Graham Ikin, Clare Cameron and Derek Neville, all of them prolific and successful writers. Apart from his international subscribers, Hamblin had close ties to comparative spiritual thinkers in many other countries, especially in the U.S.

Although he had been brought up in a strictly religious family, he hadn't found any of the answers he sought in the Church. He realised that, rather than following any creed or dogma, which didn't work for him anyway, he had to look within himself. He found contact with 'Presence' and realised it held the key to the peace he was seeking. All the time, his search was leading him nearer to discovering the way his thoughts affected his performance and outlook.

During the General Strike of 1926, the Great Depression of 1929-32, and again in years after the end of the Second World

War, many homeless, unemployed wayfarers came to the Hamblin household seeking relief and shelter. Henry and Elizabeth provided them with a simple meal, new boots and clothing, and money for the road. Known colloquially as 'The Saint of Sussex", Hamblin was a man who applied his spiritual principles to his everyday life. Practical Mysticism was Hamblin's life's work. He helped people in deeply practical ways to become less fearful, happier, and more successful in their lives. To this end, he wrote books like *The Antidote to Worry*. However, later in life he realised that whilst these books genuinely helped people, they were largely concerned with the personality. He then wished to go a step further and become more fully a truly 'practical mystic', so he wrote a spiritual course of 26 lessons, each with a definite theme presented in a systematic way. This was designed to move beyond the constraints of personality so that the soul could breathe the pure air of Spirit. What was needed, he felt, was 'a total surrender of ourselves to the Divine.' The course is available as the book *The Way of the Practical Mystic*.

The Power of Thought

Hamblin was at the forefront of the New Thought movement which was gaining pace in the early 20th century. He discovered that 'new thought' was, in fact, ancient wisdom, based upon the truth that has always existed since before time began. All great souls give voice to that timeless truth in a myriad of different ways. Hamblin urges us to "Think in harmony with the Universal

Mind." In other words, he underlines the fact that truth is and cannot be changed depending upon our mood or our whim.

Hamblin realised that we need not only a positive frame of mind but an applied way of thinking - Right Thinking, as he termed it. What did he mean by that? Well, he wrote a book on it, *The Little Book of Right Thinking*, which is in its 17th reprint. Essentially, he defines Right Thinking as:

- Thinking from the Divine standpoint.

- Controlling the thoughts so they do not go off on negative tangents away from the Divine Truth, which is always positive.

- Replacing negative thoughts with positive thoughts

- Living in the consciousness that all is well; and as an adjunct to this, remembering that perfection exists as a reality now, and to think in the consciousness of that knowledge.

- Meditation or prayer is the highest form of Right Thinking.

- Ultimately, however, the aim is to get beyond thought, 'to enter ultimate Truth'.

He says, 'When we cease thinking, we glide out on the ocean of God's Peace. Thought brings us to the foot of the mountain after which we have to proceed by intuition'.

> *'Health, Wealth and Happiness. Isn't this something we all want, either for ourselves or for those dear to us? And yet, how many of us are struggling to reach or hold such a goal for a sustained period of time?'*

Hamblin's teachings explain how we can achieve all of these things, not by hard work and striving but by a simple change of thought. *Within You is the Power* is one of his simple but profound statements, and the title of one of his books.

Hamblin was a prolific author and had many thousands of followers studying and benefiting from his teachings and courses until his death in 1958. The simple principles contained in those teachings are as relevant today as they were when he was alive, and can still help us to achieve health, prosperity and happiness if we apply them conscientiously.

He died in 1958 in Chichester Hospital. The Hamblin Trust exists to this day to propagate the legacy of his work.

The Relevance of his Teachings Today

Hamblin was, essentially, a Christian mystic, yet his ideas about the simplicity and clarity of presence seem incredibly contemporary.

He believed that the source of all wisdom is within us and all around us, and that this is the fundamental reality; there is no separation, and we are all one. His message and advice to all who read his work is that it is for everyone and is in harmony with the aspiration of all good people throughout time. Hamblin believed that there can be no finite creed of an infinite faith. Moreover, he suggests that, when creeds appear, true faith can be constrained.

He cautioned that if you seek God in prayer, the corollary is that you must have faith in Him. He often stressed that no prayer goes unanswered, and, although you may not get the answer requested, your prayer will be answered in some form. God is around us and within us, and this is the fundamental reality. He made it clear that, although human organisations come and go, God's laws are eternal, and that God is the quintessence of love, wisdom, and harmony. He expresses the clear view that "Blessed are they who believe and yet have not seen". The knowledge that God is born within us is fundamental to our understanding, and only by the loss of self can God be found. At the point a person surrenders his or her 'self' to God, it is then that a re-birth takes place and one's real life in God begins.

Some may question this view and ask: "What is this but the core teachings of the many brands of Christianity?" In response, Hamblin's view was that modern Christianity is a heterogeneous compound of the teachings of Jesus interwoven with historic pagan-based doubts and fears, litanies, supplications and more, all of which are closely guarded by a priestly hierarchy. These were strong views, and Hamblin does not disparage those who found them uncomfortable, as he says that churches are necessary and helpful for those who are succoured by them. Hamblin had a lifelong rebellious streak where authority was concerned, and this included the strictures of the Church. Hamblin would sometimes say that the Truth of the message of Jesus was so often wrapped up in dogma and creed that its purity and simplicity were obscured.

In his teaching, he states that first comes purity of intention, reminding his readers that one cannot serve God and Mammon. Either you trust God completely or you hedge your bets by having worldly alliances and a healthy bank balance. He maintains that trying to achieve both will impair spiritual development. Secondly, an individual's dedication to following God's path will require great patience, perseverance, faith and courage; but in following this path, the individual will develop forbearance and good will. He adds that other life experiences will follow naturally and lead to a developing compassion, which will enable the individual to radiate the love of God.

Where should we place Hamblin in the long line of mystics, seekers and finders? Perhaps it is rather impertinent to pose the question some 65 years after his death, but it is surely relevant to consider this point as, by any measure, he was an extraordinary person.

Remember that he was born into a life of poverty and obscurity but, despite a very limited education, by superhuman efforts of his imagination, he rose to wealth and secured an esteemed position in life, while all the time being aware of another "self" within him, a spiritual self. Dramatically, in the middle part of his life, he surrendered his material successes to follow his wider calling as a disciple of God. In this later life, he did not subscribe to any specific creed or form of religion. He was no haloed saint in the traditional sense, but he would have said, "What I have done, or rather what has been done through me, can be done by any person in the world according to their gifts and personal faith".

The essence of this teaching is that the latent power of God lies within everyone.

John Delafield is the grandson of Henry Thomas Hamblin and a retired RAF pilot. The majority of his childhood was spent living with his grandparents, Henry Thomas and Elizabeth Eva Hamblin.

Chapter One

Transforming Thought Through the Power of the Infinite

It is not sufficient for us to have aspirations after a richer and fuller life. Such aspirations are good, and without them we could make no progress at all, but we need something in addition. The whole secret is one of thought control and thought direction. Aspirations are good, because without them our thoughts could never be raised to higher and better things, but we need practical thought training in addition. Aspiration directs our thoughts upwards, but unless we have some practical method of keeping them up, they soon fall down again. Then our old habits, or ways of life, reassert themselves, our ideals become dimmed, and aspirations die away.

If, however, we can keep our thoughts up, then ideals and aspirations remain fresh and clear, thus stimulating the raising of the thoughts so that we become stronger and stronger from day-to-day. Instead of working in a vicious circle, which is the case if diffuse or uncontrolled thinking is indulged in, we travel along a spiral that leads ever upwards to higher and better things, which include self-control, liberty, freedom, achievement, overcoming, victory, and harmony and peace. If we learn to overcome our thoughts, we overcome ourselves; and if we overcome ourselves, we can rule the world. Indeed, in literal truth, we can rule our own world, and this is really the only thing that matters.

The qualifications for entering the richer and fuller new life of overcoming and victory are right aspiration and a right will, combined with elevated and controlled thinking. We already possess right aspiration and right will, otherwise we would not be studying this subject together. At one time we would not have dreamed of doing such a thing. Our tastes and inclination ran in a different direction. We have had these new aspirations born within us, which have made us heartily sick of the old life of limitation and bondage, because of attraction. The Centre of the Universe, the One Source of life, wisdom, love, and power, is a mighty magnet who is always attracting and drawing men to Himself. This attractive power makes us long for a larger, better, and fuller life altogether, than the one of weakness and limitation or mistaken direction that we may have lived in the past. Therefore, because of this attraction we now have aspirations of a higher nature and longings for things which we cannot describe.

This attraction, and these higher longings, are, however, not sufficient. We have to co-operate with the higher influences. They are very delicate and sensitive. If we do not cooperate with them, they will grow blunted and dim, finally disappearing altogether, to our internal and incalculable loss.

These higher aspirations after a better and fuller life must therefore be supplemented, upheld, and cooperated with by us. This is done by the use we make of our thoughts. Thoughts are creative, they are the root of all action and the hidden cause of all phenomena. The centre or creative source of the Universe is seeking to draw our thoughts upwards towards Himself, so that they should conform to the Divine Harmony. Infinite Wisdom, of course, knows that if our thoughts conform to the Universal Harmony they will be reinforced by Divine Power, so that our whole life will become transformed, and we, ourselves, will become so changed as to be entirely new creatures; far, far, better in every way than we can possibly dream of, or imagine, now.

We must remember, however, that it is not our thoughts, really, that accomplish this transformation, it is the *Supreme Spiritual Power of the Universe*. Through raising our thoughts, they become harmonised with the eternal, harmonious thoughts of the Infinite, and this releases the Secret Power of the Universe. At the same time, we open ourselves to receive an influx of dynamic internal life, which not only fills us with new life and power but changes us until we become new creatures. Therefore, while all this is not possible, except we continually raise our thoughts, yet it is not our thoughts that accomplish these wonders, but the Infinite Power of eternal being that is released as soon as our thoughts become harmonised with the higher vibrations.

This is rather a paradox, but it is necessary for us to bear it in mind, always. *We are greatly privileged in being called to this greater and fuller life* and it is of the utmost importance that we cooperate with the influences that are seeking to draw us upwards.

Now, not only are our own thoughts incapable of accomplishing that which we desire, but it is also equally true that our own will of itself, cannot do all that we wish it to do. Why so many of us fail is that we think we can accomplish our right thinking by sheer will-power. There is a double error here. The first error may be in thinking that we can transform ourselves and our life by the power of our thoughts and will. The will and the thoughts are inseparably bound up together, for one cannot think constructively or purposefully without the use of the will. We have already seen that it is not the power of human thought that transforms the life, but the power of the Infinite which is released on our behalf when our thoughts become harmonised with, or conjoined to, the thoughts of the Universal Supreme Mind. This applies to the will also, because the will and the thoughts are bound up together. The second error is in thinking that the human will can sustain the effort of looking up, so that the power of the Infinite can flood the life. The human will is not capable of doing so, but has to be reinforced by the greater will of the Supreme. It is because of these two errors that so many of us fail. We have born in us the desire to live a higher and finer life: we want to cultivate a fuller and richer thought-life which in time will be reflected in our outward life; but we fail, because our will is not strong enough to withstand the tremendous opposition which it encounters.

However, If, we acknowledge that our own powers are not sufficient and that it is only through the release of the Supreme Power that our life can be transformed; and also if we acknowledge that our own will is insufficient, and that the greater will of the Supreme must come to our aid if we are to remain steadfast and become victorious - if we do this, we shall not fail: you simply cannot fail, for we have behind us the whole power of the Universe. This is so because our own feeble will is reinforced and strengthened out of all knowledge by the Master Will of the Universe.

Acknowledging our own weakness and recognising that we are dependent upon a far greater power and will does not weaken our will or rob us of willpower. Just the reverse is the case. The will grows stronger the more it becomes reinforced by the will of the Supreme.

Such willpower is needed, for one who sets out to live the higher life arouses a tremendous opposition. When we start to rise all the old habits of thought and action and the whole "atmosphere", if it can be so termed, do their level best to drag us back again. It is as though we were in a deep pit with slippery sides, and that when we attempt to climb out a thousand devils cling to us and by persuasion, bullying, intimidation, petty persecutions, troubles, difficulties, and misrepresentations, do all in their power to keep us down. And the lower self also wars against the higher, and many are the enticements to lure us away from our new ideals, and deaden our aspirations, so that we need the help of a power greater than that of the finite self, and a willpower that is far greater than our own.

Those who do not acknowledge their need of a greater power and a stronger will fail in their efforts at right thinking. The power is there, but they cannot make contact. We can only be helped to the extent that we acknowledge it and surrender to it; therefore, the more we do so the greater becomes the power that is released on our behalf. This power does not work for us and then leave us as weak as before. It is incorporated with our life: it is welded into our character: it is forged into our very being, so that we become strong, steadfast, immovable.

We have, then, right aspiration and the right will, but we need power to overcome, and strength to reinforce our will. The first comes to us through raising our thoughts, and by acknowledging that our own power is insufficient. As we do this an influx of Infinite Life and Power flows into us. The second is by acknowledging that our own will is insufficient, and that the Will of the Supreme, working through our will, is necessary.

A kind of spiritual perpetual motion is thus put into action. By raising our thoughts, we release inexhaustible power. This power enables us to keep on raising our thoughts, even when our own powers are exhausted. This enables us to draw fresh power from the Infinite, so that instead of our powers being exhausted, they become greater and greater.

INFINITE MIND
SUPER-CONSCIOUS MIND
CONSCIOUS MIND
WILL

Explanation:

Through the exercise of the will, we can raise our consciousness to the realm of the super- conscious and thus employ a stratum of mind that is above ordinary consciousness. This we have termed the super-conscious mind. This higher stratum of mind is in touch with the Infinite Mind. Every time that we raise our thoughts to the super-conscious plane, realm, or strata, we open ourselves to an influx of power from the Infinite Mind. This enables us to keep on raising the thoughts in spite of everything that would try to pull them down. Every time that we raise our thoughts, we make it easier for us to do so next time. The cells of our brain which have been used for wrong thinking will go out of commission, while new brain cells used exclusively for right-thinking will come into cultivation and become filled with energy.

Summary:

- Right will and aspiration must be supplemented by control of the thoughts.

- Thoughts, that is, human thoughts, cannot of themselves transform the life, but by raising them, Infinite Power flows into the life.

- The human will is not sufficient to withstand the opposition met with, but by acknowledging a greater will the human will is reinforced by the will of the Supreme.

- The power of the Infinite is incorporated with our being and the strength of the Supreme Will welded into our human will.

- A spiritual perpetual motion is set in action; power from the Infinite enabling us to keep on keeping on in spite of great opposition. Every effort makes us stronger.

Conclusion

Study this lesson every day. Make use of the following affirmation whenever you think of it. Think quietly of it as you fall asleep, but only if it does not excite you or make you wakeful.

> I raise my thoughts to a higher plane and am filled with infinite power.

You may wonder how you are to raise your thoughts to a higher plane before being taught. You may also say that you cannot do so because of the cares and worries of this life. This is the first piece of wrong thinking that you have the privilege of overcoming. Instead of saying or thinking: "I cannot raise my thoughts", or "how can I raise my thoughts to a higher plane when I have so much care and worry?", you will say, calmly and quietly and dispassionately, "I raise my thoughts to a higher plane, and am filled with Infinite Power".

Of course, in subsequent lessons, you will receive plenty of further instruction, but this statement alone will help you considerably. Through it you will find it comparatively easy to think above the petty annoyances, conceits, and mean happenings of life. It will also enable you to rise above the fears to which most people are subject. Meet everything with the affirmation given in this lesson and you will become conscious of a new and wonderful power that is within you.

You must, however, not be satisfied with reading this lesson and then casting it aside. It should be read daily and thought over. Also, the affirmation must be USED, and not merely read.

Chapter Two

Empowering Visualisations and Affirmations

We are endeavouring to put the teaching of this course on a higher plane than any popular or so-called practical psychological teaching with which we are acquainted, and therefore you will find that it differs from the latter in many ways. It is advisable at this point to show in what way, in two main aspects, it differs from the usual teaching along these lines.

Firstly: the student is generally taught to form an image in the mind of wealth, lovely surroundings, or any other desired state, and to concentrate upon it and "will" it into manifestation. This is a mild form of black magic. If a person is good at visualising and strong in will, such a feat can be accomplished. But the final result is disastrous and often terrible. We have in the past taught visualising as an aid to strengthening the mind, the imagination, concentration and so on. This is legitimate, but to misuse the mind and will in the way previously described is the very antithesis of our teaching.

I must mention, in passing, that the wrong psychology endeavours to change environment by mental force. The only psychology that is right, i.e. in harmony with eternal truth and the inner laws of life, teaches just the reverse. The only way is to become changed in ourselves. If we become changed for the better, our environment alters accordingly. Environment is only an effect - the cause is within. When we become changed within, our outward circumstances become changed also, or else in some way our life becomes harmoniously adjusted. We can become changed within only by a change of thought. If we change our thoughts, polarising them and bringing them into harmony with eternal law, then we can safely leave our environment to take care of itself. The life follows the thought. If we keep our thoughts up, then the life follows suit. If we look after the cause the effect must follow.

This is a most important point and must be thoroughly understood. Because it is not recognised, thousands of people who are practising mental science, New Thought, and other cults are doomed to disappointment and failure. So long as we think that we are all right and that our environment is all wrong, so long shall we be unsuccessful in our efforts to live a more harmonious life. What we must acknowledge is that we are out of harmony both with our environment and the source of our life and all life. True success and a full and abundant life can result only through a complete harmonious adjustment, both within our environment and Divine Source. For this to become possible, various changes must be made within us, through certain changes in thought and outlook.

When we realise and acknowledge all this, we are then ready to make real and substantial progress in the things that really matter.

Secondly: it is generally told that students should say: "I am success", "I am health", "I am power", and so on. This is certainly better than saying or thinking: "I am a failure", "I am ill", "I am weak", but it is far from being the highest form of teaching. It does very well for beginners for a time. In my most elementary book *Look Within* such suggestions are given, but while they appear to strengthen and certainly encourage a weak beginner for a time, they must, if real progress is to be made, be superseded by affirmations more in harmony with real or absolute Truth. The "I am" type of affirmation leads either to failure or to a gross form of egoism. For instance, incredible though it may appear, there are many misguided people today who affirm "I am God", or "I am Christ". This, of course, is the logical outcome of using the "I am" type of affirmation. Therefore, the beginner who is using it is advised to practise something better as soon as possible.

It is possible to polarise the thoughts in the highest possible manner without making use of the "I am" type of affirmation at all. The "I am" type of affirmation, while it may polarise the thoughts, inflates the personal ego, or selfhood, to such an extent as to produce the most extraordinary egoism. It also often leads to a fall, such as that of Humpty Dumpty of nursery rhyme fame. Not only can the thoughts be polarised without using "I am" affirmations, but they can be polarised very much better without them.

I do not mean, of course, that the words "I am" are to be dispensed with altogether. It is the misuse of the words that has to be avoided. It is the affirmations which arrogate to ourselves the qualities of the Infinite Mind that ought to be avoided, such as I am success, I am health, I am spirit, I am life, I am strength, I am perfect, and so on. It is not the use of the words "I am" that is wrong, but arrogating to ourselves the things, qualities or powers which alone come from God. It does not, however, matter if we do use the words "I am" so long as we put God first and acknowledge that all good things, qualities, and powers come from this Central Source.

For instance, St. Paul said: "I can do all things through Christ which strengtheneth me". This would have been an arrogant assumption on his part if he had not qualified it by acknowledging the Source of his power to overcome every difficulty and trial. Again, in our first lesson, I gave you an affirmation, "I raise my thoughts to a higher plane, and I am filled with Infinite Power". This affirmation is quite legitimate because it acknowledges that we receive the power from a Higher Source. Its meaning is that because we raise our thoughts to God, the One Source of all good and power, we become filled with a power that is not our own.

You will see how different this is from saying: "I am power". Such an assertion, while it inflates man's personal ego, or self, cuts him off from the only Source of real and infinite power. Therefore, by using the affirmation, "I am power", a student does not make himself any stronger, although he may think and feel that he is strengthened thereby. Such affirmations, as I have already said, have a limited use with raw beginners, but only for a time. From the foregoing you will see why it is that I am so anxious to get students to make use of a better form of affirmation that is entirely in harmony with the truth and laws of eternal being.

Further, whatever our religious beliefs may be, we have to acknowledge that all good things, qualities, and powers come from God, that is, from one Supreme Creative Centre. There is, in the last analysis, only one Source from which all power and goodness proceed. If people do not acknowledge this, thinking that power and goodness have their source in their personalities, they must of necessity suffer from weakness. In the first place, by their refusal to acknowledge the Source of all power and goodness, they cut themselves off from the only Source from which they can obtain power. Secondly, by their assumption that they themselves are the source of power and goodness they lay themselves open to temptations of various kinds, the power of old habits, and to various destructive forces.

What are called the dark forces have power on their own plane. So long as we rely on our own strength, that of the personal "I am" or selfhood, we are at their mercy. When, however, we look to God, the one omnipotent power, and invoke His aid, we become protected and helped by invisible forces. We may be assaulted and tried, in every possible way, but if we are steadfast, perseveringly keeping our thoughts up, we are brought safely through, becoming one of the comparatively few conquerors.

There is another aspect of this subject to which attention must briefly be called. It may be possible that one can develop his egoism along the "I am" lines arrogating to himself all power, wisdom, etc, claiming himself to be equal with God, and in time to become a very powerful ego. I do not know if this is the case. It is said by some that it is possible to develop as far along the dark path of arrogance as it is possible to travel along the path of light, love and surrender to the Will of God, even to the attainment of a state of four dimensional or universal consciousness.

If such be the case, then it makes no difference, finally; for all such power has no life in it and must ultimately be overthrown. "Every plant, which my Heavenly Father hath not planted, shall be rooted up". Matt. 15, v.13.

We will next consider where the science of right thought starts.

First, we have to get into harmony with the One Centre or Source of all life, wisdom, love, intelligence, and power. Next, we have to become harmonised with our environment and our fellow humans. We have to become harmonised with them, rather than them to us. In other words, we have to react harmoniously to our environment. We have to cooperate with life as we find it, instead of fighting against it. Just as nature can be overcome only to the extent that we obey her laws, so also can we overcome our life's difficulties only by working in harmony with life's experiences and in correspondence with our environment.

Thinking, then, must start with the one creative centre *or* Source. Not I or self, but God.

What do we mean by the word God?

To me the word means far more than I can ever express in words or even thought, but as far as this course of lessons is concerned, we mean by the term God principally *omnipotence*.

Let me say, in passing, that this is not a course in theology or even metaphysics. By *omnipotence* we mean the supreme, creative, active, ruling power of life and the universe. We are not teaching absolutism. If you are anxious about the Christology of our teaching, I refer you to the first few verses of the first chapter of St. John's gospel, and this, I think, will put your mind at rest.

There is only one omnipotent power in the universe. What are called the powers of darkness, or evil, are not omnipotent. They can affect us only to the extent that we fail to make contact with *omnipotence*. The power of *omnipotence* is unlimited and infinite. The powers of darkness are limited and circumscribed. The powers of evil appear to be infinite and unlimited, but this is not the case, for they can function only on lower planes.

When we rise to higher planes of thought we find that their evil has no power: it cannot function on higher spiritual planes of being. Therefore, the powers of darkness and evil are not omnipotent: they are limited and circumscribed.

The one and only omnipotent power is that of God.

We must therefore place first in all that we say and think *God*.

We must not say: "I am Life" but "God is my life". We must not say: "I am power", but "God is Power in me".

Whatever your need may be, you can affirm that the One Omnipotent God is your source and supply. When you use reverently the word God think of universal, inexhaustible, omnipotent power. By using this word you invoke the only omnipotence, the only omnipotent power.

Now having got a comprehensive idea of what is implied by the word God you can add the words "is my ---", filling in whatever your need may be.

You will thus be calling upon *omnipotence* and invoking the only *power* and this can never be exhausted and can never fail.

Man can gain nothing by using "I am" affirmations, for if he does so he simply travels in a circle and remains as far away from life and power as before. He can only benefit by looking straight to the One Centre and by acknowledging that everything that he needs comes from this centre which is God.

In thinking of God as *omnipotence*, we of course must not forget that He is also *infinite love, mercy, wisdom, intelligence, knowledge, mind*, and so on. He is all that we intuitively know to be good, beautiful, and true to an infinite degree.

> God Is my Refuge,
> God is my Strength,
> God is my Deliverer,
> God is my Shield,
> God is my All in All.

Christ said: "And I give unto them eternal life; and they shall never perish, neither shall any pluck them out of my hand".

CHAPTER THREE

Finding The Good in Life

The great secret of a perfect life is the cultivation of unity and adjustment. Until we learn this great lesson we fill our life with discord, friction and disharmony.

Although it may seem simple to you and of no importance it is a great, arcane, inner, hidden truth (which but few people seem to discover or follow) that we do not have to fight against our environment but become adjusted to it. A very wise man said to me the other day: "Man dies because he is out of harmony with his environment". A great writer on recondite subjects says: "It is a question of adaptability to environment, which must go on until the end. Ill health, disease, and death are effects immediately due to lack of this power of adaptation". I do not profess to be able to tell you how to avoid physical death, but I **can** tell you how to become so adjusted through life's experiences as to enter into liberty and freedom.

What we all have to learn is that life is good and not evil, and that all its experiences have for their sole object our highest well-being. Because of this it is folly to fight against life and its experiences and discipline; for by so doing, we fight against our highest good, and even against God.

This is a great and fundamental **truth**, therefore let us get hold of it very firmly and clearly.

Life is good and all its experiences must be cooperated with.

If we examine our life in the light of this truth, we shall probably find that, in a hundred different ways, we are at loggerheads with it. We have probably already found out that it is impossible to avoid the disciplines of life, but we may resent them all the same. We may say, perhaps, with resignation: "What cannot be cured must be endured", but, all the time, we may not be in willing cooperation with it all. So long as there is this lack of cooperation we are out of adjustment with our environment, we are not in harmony with life itself, or with its Divine purpose.

Our religious leaders teach us resignation. We must be resigned to the will of God, they tell us. This is better than rebelling against it, but it is not sufficient. For instance, it implies, to a certain extent, that life and the will of God are miserable and unhappy experiences which must be endured somehow. What is needed, really, is a belief that life and the will of God are good, together with willing co-operation, on our part, with them, gladly, joyfully.

If we do this we pass more quickly through our trouble or difficulty, and enter into liberty, freedom and peace.

Instead of being resigned, in a negative and hopeless way, to the will of God, lying down in misery, awaiting fresh "afflictions", we should rise up gladly, co-operating with the glorious will of God which desires for us only good, and nothing but good.

When we believe that life and its experiences are good, to be co-operated with willingly, joyfully and happily, we become more adjusted to life; we come more into harmony with our environment.

The great, inner secret is that life is friendly and good and is always trying to help us and to teach us something with as little suffering and unpleasantness as possible. The lessons have to be learnt, but instead of learning them unwillingly and painfully, we can learn them willingly and pleasantly.

Therefore, the first step is to believe that life is good and that all its experiences are good. One who realises this truth becomes transformed in outlook and his life becomes changed also. So long as we believe life to be evil, it IS evil, to us. Everything that is dark, gloomy, sinister, miserable, drab, unpleasant, becomes magnified and emphasised out of all proportion, so that life appears to be a very evil thing. We then see life through distorted eyes, and it looks very evil indeed but when we believe life to be good, and if we look for the good in circumstances and people, we find so much good on every hand that we are overwhelmed with the wonder of it. Actually, also, life does become far more harmonious, simply because the discordant element has been removed.

Not only is there this inherent goodness in life and its experiences, this same "good" is inherent in our fellow creatures. Some may think it is silly and childish to look for more good in people than is apparent. But it is not silly or childish, it is the deepest and highest wisdom. If we look for the good, we find it; which only shows that it must have been there all the time, although we could not see it until we searched for it.

Let me attempt to illustrate this. If we walk along a country lane, unobservantly, we see nothing but a few fields and hedges. If, however, we observe and examine the hedgerows in detail, we find so much beauty as to amaze us and overwhelm us. We are quite overcome by the wonders that are revealed to us, but which are hidden from the usual glance of the average person. A new world of beauty and delight is opened to us, simply through looking for the beauty which before lay hidden.

It is the same with good in other people. It may lie hidden, covered by many a surface fault or strange twist or blemish, but the true gold is there, nevertheless. If we look for it, we truly find it.

What is needed from us is unity and adjustment. The worst thing possible is to rebel against life's experiences. Through thinking they are evil we naturally are inclined to rebel against them, or, upon finding that this is useless, to pity ourselves as being ill-used or "hard done by".

Life is good. If we pity ourselves, we only make the apparent evil worse. If life's experiences are too much for us, it shows that we are dealing with them in the wrong way, that we are out of adjustment.

I am trying very hard to explain one of the greatest truths possible, which, when apprehended, entirely changes the life.

If we are not to be broken up by life, but instead are to be greatly enriched by its experiences, we must be *flexible*.

Perhaps you have seen the picture which shows a terrific gale uprooting the stubborn oak, but which is only able to bend the gentle unresisting grass. After the storm is over the grass is just the same as before, but the proud oak tree lies prostrate on the ground, never to rise again.

This picture represents a deep truth, the truth of *flexibility*. If we are flexible, as far as life's experiences, tests and trials are concerned, like the gentle unresisting grass, we rise again when the storm has passed, uninjured by all that we have passed through. If, however, we are stubborn, or if we resist, or pity ourselves through thinking that life's tests and disciplinary experiences are evil, then we are liable to be broken or uprooted in the storms of life.

We all have to pass through storms, trials, tests and searching experiences, and, if we are flexible and unite with them, we become greatly enriched in character, entering that state of calm, repose, peace, happiness and harmony to which only a few attain. We **have** to pass through these experiences, everything depends upon **how** we meet them.

You may wonder where psychology comes in, or to what extent Right Thinking is involved in the teaching of this lesson.

The object of this lesson is to gain an insight into life, so that we think rightly from conviction and understanding, instead of attempting to do so simply because we are taught to do so.

If we believe that life is good and not evil, the whole current of our thought becomes changed, and consequently every action and decision is affected. Our thought becomes truly optimistic in place of pessimistic, and because of this we succeed, in the highest and truest sense of the word, where otherwise we would fail. By thinking rightly and by being *flexible* we are filled with power, so that we are able to exhibit all the strength and patience that are necessary for victory, and yet so to "give" to the storms of life as to keep ourselves from being broken, uprooted, or crushed. In consequence we are led into the only path that can bring us to calm, peace, joy and true satisfaction.

The first step, then, is to believe that life is good, and that all its experiences, tests and trials are for our real and highest good. Behind the "good" of the ordinary life is a larger "good", of which we become aware, more and more clearly as we progress along the true, inner path of life. But this does not imply outward evil. While we must be prepared to surrender temporary or partial good for the sake of the larger good; yet, strange though it may seem, if we seek the latter at the expense of the former, then the best in this life becomes ours. "Seek ye first the Kingdom of God and His righteousness, (the larger good) and all these things (the lesser good) shall be added unto you".

This is a great paradox, but in it is to be found the key to an endless and richer and fuller life.

But, you may say, how can I believe that life is good and that it is friendly, always trying to help me; while I am confronted with every possible evil and difficulty? Or it may be that you are concerned more about the troubles and sufferings of others. How, you say, can life be good, and how can I believe it to be good?

There is a simple and direct path, which, if followed, brings us not only to belief, but also to understanding. And the simple, direct way is to make use of two affirmations.

The first is: **Life is good.**

The second is: **Nothing but good can come to me.**

If we keep on using these, we gradually grow or expand into a new consciousness. We understand and realise interiorly and in spite of the intellect, that life is good and that all things are conspiring together to bring about our highest and eternal good.

Through using these affirmations, we come to believe that life's experiences are good; then, through this belief, we naturally desire to co-operate with life instead of rebelling against its experiences. This in time transforms our life, for we work in harmony with Divine Law and the Divine Plan.

In this way we become flexible instead of stubborn; thus, bending to the storm instead of being broken by it. We come into unity with life, thus entering into harmony and peace.

CHAPTER FOUR

Learning Through Non-Resistance From Letting Go

In your last lesson you were introduced to one of the most arcane truths, over which the worldly wise in all ages have stumbled, and which has only been accepted by the spiritually wise and illumined. It was the burden of the teaching of Jesus, and if only people had followed it, they would have been saved from much suffering, and the world would have been led in the way of harmony and peace, instead of into war and all its attendant suffering.

This truth is **non-resistance**.

Now to most people this doctrine is absolute foolishness, while to a smaller number it is a very beautiful but impossible and remote ideal. Few people can see how such a teaching can be followed in the world today, but you will realise, as this lesson unfolds that it is not only possible, but it is also the only way to victory, overcoming and complete emancipation.

I must explain, however, what is meant by non-resistance. We will do this, first of all, by pointing out what it is *not*. Non-resistance does not mean that we are to allow ourselves to be led into sin. It does not mean that we are to allow evil thoughts to enter our mind. It does not mean that we are to stand by and see injustice done to others, without protest on our part. It does not mean that we are to allow the weak and helpless to be injured or bullied without attempting to defend them. It does not mean that we are not to overcome in the battle of life.

Non-resistance does mean, however, that we are not to resist or rebel against the disciplinary experiences in our own life. It means also that we are not to retaliate when wronged, and that we must not try "to get our own back" when hurt or injured by others. It also means that we do not *fight* temptation or evil habit, in the ordinary sense, that is in our own finite strength but overcome in quite a different way. (This, however, will be dealt with in a separate lesson.)

All this is quite enough for most people, but, to the more advanced soul, *non-resistance* means loving one's enemies and those who persecute us or slander us. It means allowing all the powers of evil to have their way with us, for it is only by so doing that we can attain to the higher consciousness and enter into full liberty and freedom.

What Jesus meant by not resisting evil was doubtless mainly that we are not to resist or avoid persecution for the sake of our religion and principles; but the same truth is applicable to other experiences. That this is so the teaching of this lesson will show.

Before we can understand the principle of non-resistance, we must know something of life itself.

Life is an experience and training, and the Spirit, that is God, is our constant teacher. This teaching comes through the experiences of life. These experiences come through people as well as events. When we meet with opposition, disappointment, injustice (to ourselves), cruelty (to ourselves), difficulty of any kind, these are not things to be cursed but are educative experiences which have for their object the building up in us of nothing less than the *divine character*. When we meet with someone who is "nasty" to us, or when we are wronged, the natural feeling is to retaliate. But the "natural" feeling is not the way of the Spirit: it is not the way of Life, but of death.

Getting one's own back is very "natural", but it perpetuates the trouble. Also, it prevents all who indulge in it from making any progress towards liberty and freedom. Such a one simply stays in the darkness, never becoming free from the trouble and venom and spitefulness of life.

Now it is a great arcane truth, a full explanation of which can be found in the deeper and more abstruse works of Jacob Boehme, that those who set out on the path of the New Life (the life lived in harmony with divine, eternal, immutable law) have to work their way through a period of darkness. Jacob himself terms it "the wrath and the darkness", but he does not mean by this the wrath of an angry and jealous God. What he does mean cannot be explained here fully, but it will be sufficient if we look upon it as a period of testing and trial through which we **must** pass if we are to arrive at the stage of true liberty and freedom.

As all of us who essay to climb the steep path which leads to emancipation and freedom have to pass through trying times, the most important thing for us is how to meet these tests and experiences in such a way as to bring us through, not only safely, but as rapidly as possible.

The only way is by non-resistance. If we look upon our difficulties or apparent calamities not only as something that **must** be passed through, but as something that is going to provide us with most valuable and helpful experience, we find it easy to cooperate with life instead of opposing it. Instead of trying to avoid the trouble or test that lies before us, the way of wisdom is to rest and rely on a power greater than our own and then to go forward determined to extract as many lessons as possible from what lies before us.

By being **willing** to pass through all experiences we escape most of the suffering. Suffering is mostly in the mind. The more we rebel against an experience, the greater the tension becomes and consequently the more acute the suffering. As soon as we relax and let go, ceasing to resist, we find that what we have to pass through is much easier to bear than we imagined.

It must be mentioned in passing that by thought control and by thinking positively instead of negatively, a tremendous amount of trouble is avoided. Speaking generally, most of the troubles of life are self-created by wrong thinking and by an inward pessimism. These are avoided, to a very large extent, by right thinking, and by the development of a strong character, and by living a life of courage and good will. Everyone must be trained and disciplined, however, so that there are experiences and difficulties which have to be met and overcome or passed through. But whatever may be the cause of our trouble or difficulty, the remedy is the same, as this teaching will clearly show.

It is not easy at first to allow life to push us about anyhow and anywhere, just as it pleases. It is so natural and so nice to fight; but doing so leads only to further enslavement and difficulty. Non-resistance at first makes one feel so helpless, but after a time we find that it is leading us to harmony and peace. For instance, let us suppose that you want a certain house, but someone, to your great annoyance, prevents you from occupying it. You *want* to fight this person, but instead you "let him go". Afterwards you find that if you had fought the case and got possession it would have been the worst thing possible for you, as it would have kept you from something far better. The resistance that we imagine you met with was not evil, it was Infinite Wisdom stopping you in one direction in order that you might go in a much better one.

Again, because you are spiritually minded and have no liking for foolish or vain things, you may be persecuted by your acquaintances. They may jeer at and mock you because of your love of good and truth. If you resist this, and rebel against it, not outwardly, perhaps, but only in your heart, you will suffer acutely, and also your witness will not be a true one. If, however, you "let them go" mentally, ceasing all resistance, you enter into peace. Also, your witness becomes a true and faithful one and must be the means of blessing others.

It must not be thought for a moment that non-resistance implies weakness. Far from it, it calls for the utmost courage and endurance. It means going forward, willing to take all that comes, rather than shirk ever so little of the experience. It means, very often, taking a very difficult and unpleasant path of duty, in preference to an apparently pleasant path of ease and pleasure. It means "taking one's medicine"; it means "facing the music"; it means welcoming all life's experiences without whining, without complaint, without rebellion, without fear.

Behind all life's experiences stands infinite and eternal love. It does not matter how cruel life may appear to be; this truth remains. It is all Love, from birth to the end. Because of this, all things conspire together to bring about our highest good, our eternal joy.

The saddest cases I have ever known in connection with my work have been those who rail at life, and what they believe to be its injustices. If they had only known, as it has been given to me to know, that all is Love, and that life desires for us only our highest good, they would have thought rightly, in harmony with this truth, and thus their life would have become transformed.

Now, dear student, the points that we have to emphasise in connection with this Lesson are these:

> *God is love.*
> *Life is love's expression.*
> *Life, because it is good, must be co-operated with, instead of resisted.*

What all this amounts to is this: we must allow life to have its way with us, no matter how difficult, hard or unfair its dealings with us may appear to be. We must not resist or fight those who wrong or injure us. We must mentally let them go. In our natural state we mentally hold them in bondage. The way of the spirit is to "loose them and let them go".

No matter how much you may be wronged, no matter with what ingratitude you meet, no matter how unjust the treatment you receive, do not let it rankle, do not let it make you rebel and resist, but just let it all go, let them all go.

If you do this, you will become detached, and you will enter into peace and freedom.

Let them all go, with their venom, their selfishness, their squabbles, their strivings, their envy, their injustices. They cannot hurt you if you do not resist. As soon as you "let go" you enter into freedom.

Is this easy? No, but it **can** be accomplished. As soon as the binding thought of resentment or resistance comes you can remember this lesson, saying to yourself:

"I let them all go, I lift my attention to higher and better things, to love, harmony, peace, joy and infinite good".

There is a higher stratum of thought to which you can raise your consciousness. By making use of positive words which represent positive ideas you help your consciousness to rise. Such words are God-words, words representing Divine Ideas, therefore they have power - vibratory power.

If you wish to rise in consciousness to this higher plane, try to lift yourself upwards, at the same time saying, "harmony, peace, love and joy", over and over again. You can also say when vexed:

> *I forgive all*
> *I love all*
> *I turn my attention to: -*
> *Love, joy, peace*
> *Harmony, infinite*
> *Perfection and good.*

By this simple practise of switching over, your thoughts will be trained into fresh channels; the old cells used by wrong thinking will die away, and new cells used for thinking thoughts of love, cooperation, peace, joy and harmony will be brought into action in their place. These new cells will be charged with energy, so that they can instantly be used for the thinking of right thoughts instead of the old thoughts which used to destroy.

The thoughts that are represented by the words ***love, joy, peace, forgiveness, harmony*** are Life and Incorruption. The thoughts opposite to these are those of death and corruption.

Afterword

It is not sufficient to read this lesson and to say: "Yes, it is a very beautiful ideal and I believe in it". Its teaching must be put into practice. There must be a constant switching over of the thoughts, as well as a non-resistance. Not only is it necessary to meet life's experiences with co-operation, it is also equally important that the eyes should be raised to the eternal hills of God. The words peace, love, harmony, goodwill, all represent God. They are the hills of God. By repeating them you will be raised in consciousness to a higher plane, "to breathe the sweet aether blowing of the breath of God". (Edward Carpenter).

CHAPTER FIVE

Harmony And Peace Through Love and Forgiveness

This brings us naturally to the subject of forgiveness. You may wonder what this may have to do with right thinking or psychology. It has everything to do with it, for we cannot think aright until we learn to forgive. All thinking that takes place while we are unforgiving is wrong thinking, and therefore destructive, leading to corruption and death.

Jesus taught the most staggering and fundamental truths in a few simple words. He seemed to lay no special stress on them, yet they are so great and wonderful, even a lifetime of study and exposition could never exhaust them. One of the greatest things he taught was this: "Forgive us our trespasses even as (or exactly as) we forgive (or have forgiven) them that trespass against us". Later Jesus amplifies this by saying: "For if you forgive men their trespasses, your Heavenly Father will also forgive you: but if ye forgive not men their trespasses, neither will your Father forgive your trespasses.

This is the tremendous and fundamental truth - a truth that goes down to the very beginnings and foundations of all life and conduct - stated in a few simple words, almost without comment. I suppose it is because of this that the world has passed it by.

What Jesus taught is that God is love and is forgiveness itself. We cannot, however, enter into the atmosphere of the Divine Presence where alone is harmony, peace, joy, and all good, until we, too, are filled with love and forgiveness towards our neighbour. It rests with us whether we enter into peace or not. The door is always open, but we cannot enter so long as we love sin or are unforgiving towards those who have wronged us.

We all of us know that it is only as we repent of all that we have done wrong in the past, all the mistakes we have made, and all the evil which we have wrought, it is only then that we get rid of its burden. It is only when we repent, deeply and truly, that we can start the new life. I am not going to say anything more about this, because the repentance stage must have been passed in your case, otherwise you would not be taking this course of lessons. Of course, we all repent daily of our shortcomings and failings, but this is not the great act of repentance and surrender to which I have referred.

Repentance and turning to God admit us into the outer courts, so to speak, but we cannot enter into the inner holy of holies until we have forgiven all trespasses against us. When we have forgiven completely and fully, we are not only in a tranquil state of mind and soul, but we are in a fit state to enter into the atmosphere of Heaven and the saints, which is harmony, peace, love, joy, and more. In the words of Jesus, our Heavenly Father forgives us exactly as we forgive others. I find it difficult to make myself clear on this point, but I hope you will see that we can enter Heaven (and this is principally a state of consciousness) only to the extent that we correspond to the atmosphere of Heaven. While it is true that we continue to live on the earth-plane, yet it is possible for us to be Heavenly minded, and thus to be Heavenly men and women.

You will see clearly that we cannot be Heavenly minded if we owe other people a grudge, or if we are unforgiving, even in the slightest degree. We can be Heavenly minded only to the extent that we love one another and forgive one another.

It is not only necessary that we refrain from hate, unforgiveness, resentment, etc., for this, after all, is only negative. It is of equal or even greater importance that we *actively* love and forgive all who have injured or wronged us. It is necessary that the whole of our thought-life should be based upon love and forgiveness. This may seem to us to be an impossible ideal at present. It is true that it may not be possible of attainment now but can be aspired after until it is attained to. When our whole thought-life becomes based upon love and forgiveness, we enter into harmony and peace.

What our soul really longs for is harmony and peace, rest and tranquillity, in God. This state of soul becomes possible only to the extent that we forgive all who have ruffled us, everything, even the slightest wrong others may have done to us. This does not mean mere negative banishing of the matter from our mind, but a free and full forgiveness, accompanied by active love and goodwill.

How can this be accomplished? By the use of thought and word. If we **say** that which we, in our best moments, really **want** to do, but which may seem impossible at present, we find that it becomes possible in course of time. If we find or make time to be quite alone and quiet, think calmly over the matter, and then, mentally addressing the one who has to be forgiven, say:

I forgive you (name of the person here) fully and freely and desire for you every possible good.

If we will do this sincerely and persistently then we find that it becomes, in time, much easier to forgive.

Time to time a student may write to us, saying that he or she **cannot** forgive certain people. Others say that they find it very difficult to forgive certain things. In all such cases the complaints are from students who have made little or no progress. Some people will take up the most advanced teaching, before they have learnt to forgive, and then wonder why they make no progress. It is, of course, impossible to make any progress towards a richer and fuller life until one learns to forgive to the uttermost, for the simple reason that one does not enter the Path that leads to Life until one does forgive. I have more than once been more than astonished at the casual remarks made by students in their letters. For instance, one student who was taking very advanced teaching, which was meant only for those who were well on the Path, and who professed to be more than ready for it, remarked casually as a sort of afterthought or aside, in a letter, that she found it very difficult to forgive some people certain things. It was said in such a way as to convey the impression that what she meant was that she could never do *that*, and therefore it was useless to talk about it. This student's letter showed clearly that she had never entered the Path at all, and that the teaching of Jesus was a sealed book to her. Yet when I gently suggested that she should discontinue the lessons because the teaching was too advanced for her, she was very indignant and told me that she had studied the teachings of much greater people than such an insignificant creature as Henry Thomas Hamblin. No doubt she had, but unfortunately her study had not done her any good, as her letter clearly showed.

We can make no progress at all towards liberation and freedom and a richer, fuller and more abundant life until we have learnt to forgive.

On the other hand, there are students who are indignant with me for daring to teach them to forgive. They say that they do not need to forgive, because they bear no one any malice. This may be true, but while they may not bear malice, yet they certainly do not *actively* love and forgive. They simply dismiss certain people from their mind, mentally writing them off as not worthy of notice. They refuse to acknowledge their injury, but in so doing they also destroy or wipe out of memory the one who committed it, as being beneath their dignity. This is very far from the active loving forgiveness which must be exercised.

Such students will never enter into harmony, peace, liberty and freedom, until they bring out again the skeleton they have hidden in their cupboard and have freely and actively forgiven in love all the injury that has been done them.

In concluding this lesson, there is one very important thing that I want to say to you, and this is: -

Let not the sun go down on your wrath

Never, on any account, and in no circumstances, retire to rest until you have forgiven fully and freely whoever may have upset you during the day. This is most important, for if you sleep on your wrath, or resentment, or feeling of injury or hurt, it will be many times more difficult to forgive, the next day, no matter how much you may try.

Before daring to go to sleep keep on with the exercise given in this lesson until you really do forgive and really mean what you say. When this is accomplished, you will enter into peace.

Every time that you overcome in this way you will win the greatest victory of life.

Additional advice

You may, of course, be "assaulted" by all kinds of thoughts of an unforgiving character: thoughts of injury and resentment. You may be tempted to allow your thoughts to dwell upon how unkindly or unjustly you have been treated, and so on. When this occurs do not allow the thoughts sufficient time in which to engage your attention; but switch over to thoughts of goodwill, forgiveness, etc. The great thing is to be quick, thus preventing the attention from being held by unworthy thoughts, suggestions and ideas.

The word "love" has been used freely in this lesson. By it I do not mean warm human affection, but goodwill, forgiveness, compassion, etc. You may use the word goodwill instead. It certainly is easier at first.

Afterword

Thinking is not only conscious, it is also subconscious, or unconscious. We may say: "I do not think such thoughts". This may be true of thoughts actively and consciously exerted or controlled by the will but may not be true of our subconscious thinking. Our hidden thoughts revolve around dominant ideas. Our hidden thoughts are creative, making or marring our life, according to their kind.

When our ideas and views change, the dominant idea in the subconscious changes also. Therefore, the character of our inner and unconscious thinking changes in correspondence.

This not only changes our life, but it also changes our very nature, because "As a man thinketh in his heart so is he". This is why advanced souls contemplate God, in order to become like Him.

It is because of this great truth that these lessons bring about unconscious right-thinking, by altering or changing the dominant idea in the subconscious mind. There can be but little really "right" thinking until this is accomplished. My object is not to give you a lot of mental exercises and gymnastics, metaphysics, etc., but to change the dominant ideas in the subconscious mind. This cannot be accomplished and right inner thinking established as a habit until every shred of unforgiveness is removed, to be replaced by **active** love, good will, forgiveness, compassion, pity and co-operation.

Love is not a negative thing, a mere absence of hate, resentment, unkindness, etc.: it is not a passive neutrality, but is a positive, live and active principle. Divine Love in us must shine and radiate like a lamp or miniature sun, blessing all with whom we come in contact. Divine Love, when truly in us, loves on, no matter how much it may be flouted and scorned. Divine Love gives and continues to give, asking nothing in return. Divine love is, in us, a well or fountain of inexhaustible pity and compassion. When we are cruelly treated, instead of hardening our heart, Love makes us say: "Father forgive them, for they know not what they do".

Chapter Six

The Secret of Unity and Harmony

Preceding lessons have brought us gradually and naturally to the very core of the teaching of Jesus. It is what He taught others to do and which He followed Himself. It is the very essence of all arcane teaching, and it is only accepted and followed by those who are spiritually advanced and who are seeking first and foremost the larger good which lies behind all lesser forms of good. The wiser, from a spiritual standpoint, a man becomes, the more readily he follows this teaching. The more foolish a man is, from the point of view of Infinite Wisdom, the more antagonistic he is towards it; in fact, he looks upon it as the greatest of all follies.

Because it has become one of the stock phrases of organised religion it may seem stale to most of us, and not of very great importance. This great teaching is that we should do the will of our Father in Heaven. Because it is a hackneyed phrase, and because it has become a platitude, it may not appeal to us very much. It is only as we follow this teaching, however, that we can become real Right Thinkers. If our thoughts are not in harmony with this truth then they are wrong thoughts, and consequently destructive. When, however, we understand what "doing the will" is we see how important it is, and how impossible it is to make any progress without it.

The Universe is one complete whole. The whole Universe emanates from one central mind and will. Because everything proceeds from this One Central Source, we each form a part of a complete Whole. Obviously, our life can become harmonious, and we can enter into unity, only if the will, purpose, design and plan of the supreme builder and architect are followed. Because there is only one designer, there can be harmony and beauty only to the extent that all parts conform to the design.

God must not be looked upon as an unreasonable despot who crushes everybody who does not conform to His Will, but rather as a Central Source of harmony and unity. God is unity, harmony and love, therefore there can be no peace or satisfaction for us if we are not in correspondence with the will, design, motive and plan of this One Central Mind, creative imagination and desire of the infinite. This is only possible to the extent that we "will" to do the will of the whole, in thought, imagination, action and desire.

Look out, in imagination, over the universe, the physical cosmos, and you will observe a most beautiful harmony, order and precision. All the heavenly bodies work together in perfect unity and cooperation. Each obeys without question the laws of the cosmos. Each follows its right path, each arrives neither one second too soon, nor one moment too late. This state of unity, harmony, precision and order is possible only because each body (some say each atom) does its right work in complete obedience to universal law and the plan of the Infinite Mind.

It will be seen that so long as this obedience and co-operation continue, the harmony and order will also continue. It will be seen also that if one of the constituent parts of the physical universe were to "go wrong", that is to disregard cosmic law and ignore the plan of the Whole, then the entire edifice would be ruined. Irregularity and destruction would spread until the whole physical Universe would become involved and crash into ruin.

It will be seen then that unity, harmony and order depend entirely upon what amounts to doing the Will of our Father in Heaven, as Jesus terms it. That is, obeying immutable law willingly, and thus helping to express the plan and purpose of the Supreme Architect.

Now the heavenly bodies, so far as I know, work obediently and harmoniously because they have no self or free will. Like a flower they obey naturally the laws which govern the Universe. Humans create discord, disaster and disorder because, through their self-will, they do not obey the laws which govern them. Unlike a planet, we are self-willed. We possess free will (within certain limits), and we use this for the self, and thus create disorder, suffering and catastrophe.

We have already seen how disastrous it would be if one of the planets, for instance, shot off on an excursion of its own, careering about the Universe according to its own ideas. This, however, is exactly what man does, and it is only through what used to be called Divine Grace - and by this we mean a healing, restraining power, influence or process, that is continually brought into operation - it is only through this that the disorder is kept from spreading beyond the confines of this planet.

The Infinite Mind, love and will desire to find expression through each of us. God's will, plan and design for each one of us is most beautiful harmonious and perfect: they can find expression only to the extent that we allow them to do so. The beauty and harmony are forever seeking to find an outlet in each one of us, but cannot do so because of "self".

It is quite impossible for anyone to live a life of harmony and peace, who does not "do the Will" of the Whole. Unless they can do this, everything is out of joint.

Those who are seeking to live their life according to higher laws do not have to fight and struggle so much as to let go, allowing Life to work through them.

"Doing the Will" is not so much doing something as allowing the Supreme Designer to arrange things for us. In course of time, we become aware of the fact that there is a perfect plan being worked out in our life: that there is a friendly, higher power working on our behalf.

The great thing is to co-operate with this plan and this friendly power. If we do not do so everything is out of joint, and what we win for ourselves can only be held or maintained by personal effort and strain.

Life becomes free from strain if we allow the plan to unfold, instead of striving and struggling to win and hold something for self.

It is exceedingly difficult to say "Thy Will be done"; but it is the essence of Right Thinking and speaking, and it leads to a life entirely free from strain and care.

You may say at this point: "How can I know which is the Will of the Whole, and which is my personal, or self, will.

It is not easy at first, but if we have a desire to do the Will of the Whole, then understanding and guidance come to us. If we live, act and decide from the standpoint of *love*, we cannot go far wrong. This helps for a time; but, if we are sincere, we next attract to us the most perplexing situations, where two or more roads, each equally right, may beckon. These perplexing situations help to develop an interior awareness and sensitiveness, which enable us to distinguish the leading of the Supreme Will and Desire.

At such times we learn to wait until the way becomes open. Then the way which opens harmoniously is always the right one.

If we have not patience enough to wait but rush off into a course of action because it appears to be the right one, or because it appeals most to self and our vanity, then we find all things out of joint. Everything goes "wrong", as we call it: everything is out of harmony.

It is the greatest mistake possible to jump to conclusions, saying that such and such things MUST be, or that we MUST have this or that, if our life is to be adjusted. The greatest mistakes that I have known people to make have been of this kind. One has said: "I must go to such and such a country, for this, that and the other reasons. It is only by this means that my life can be put right". In vain I have pleaded with them, but they have said: "You do not understand. I must etc, etc, etc". The consequence has been that they have reached the other country, only to find their difficulties much greater than before.

I have known people to say: "I MUST have certain money before my life can be put right". In spite of warnings and entreaties they have gone on and suffered very bitterly in consequence. If they have got the money they have found the bitterest sorrow in addition. If they have not obtained the money, they have been disappointed and soured.

But, in addition to all this trouble, disharmony and disappointment, there is so much strain and effort required. Whatever may be won is not only won at tremendous cost of effort but has to be maintained at even greater cost of strain, anxiety and care. In other words, one who acts in this way comes into competition with his fellow men, with life's forces, and with invisible powers. Indeed, he seems to have the whole universe against him.

But there is no strain to those who wait for the leading of the Universal Mind and Will. The Way of the Spirit is harmony and peace. Everything works smoothly like a well-oiled machine: everything comes together and fits into its proper place like a correctly assembled jigsaw puzzle. Obstacles move out of the way just at the right moment, to allow the entry of all that is good.

"Enough of this", you will say: "Now tell me how I am to do all this?"

If you have the right desire, and if you are willing to do the will of the whole you have got over the most difficult part. If, instead of saying: "I must have this or that," you pray: "Let Thy Will be done", you are already in the Path of Liberation. You can help considerably, however, if you also make use of the following statements, or the one, or more, that seem most helpful to you:

- Lead thou me on.

- I "will" to do the will of the highest.

- In times of perplexity, I wait for divine guidance.

- At all times I am guided by infinite wisdom.

- At all times I am helped by invisible forces.

- I follow the way of the spirit, which is harmony and peace.

- I have no will but thine.

Make use of those of the above which appeal to you most. When alone and quiet repeat them slowly and let them sink in. A good time is just as one is falling asleep, but all strain and tenseness must be avoided, the sentences being repeated over in a dreamy and restful manner.

CHAPTER SEVEN

Faith

Faith in God is a complete reliance upon an Omnipotent Power for Good, an infinite love, an impartial justice.

One of the principal objects of our life here is the development in us of a great faith. Indeed, one who reaches full attainment is one who learns to live a life of complete faith in God, in addition to living entirely according to the dictates of the higher law of love i.e., Love that is a blessing, a benediction, a giving out without any thought of reward or even thanks.

Because one of the principal objects of life is to teach us this great lesson, all its experiences have for their main object the cultivation and development in us of *faith*.

I have found, and am still finding, that the most difficult thing to do is really to trust God. The more that we trust God, the more we realise how little we really do trust Him. There is always an undercurrent of self-help rather than God-trust. Now self-help is an excellent thing. One of the great lessons of life is to learn to stand on one's own feet and to be self-reliant, not dependent upon other people. But after we have learned to do this, we have to learn a much greater lesson, and that is to rely entirely upon God.

In order to accomplish this, life brings us to experiences (or brings experiences to us) in which we find ourselves utterly and completely helpless. And not only so, but we also find that there is no human being who can help us. We are completely alone, entirely helpless, with no one, not even our nearest and dearest, who can help. Then we realise that there is only one who can deliver us and that is God. If then, we cast ourselves entirely upon God, in complete trust and abandonment, we find that we are delivered or brought through.

"With faith all things are possible". To the extent that we trust God the impossible becomes possible. Also, as our faith increases so are we able to rely less and less upon the methods of the world, and more and more upon Spiritual Law.

By intuition we know that the methods of the world, which are the very antithesis of love, are wrong. But the problem is: "How can we escape from them, or avoid them?" How can we do without the grabbing, grasping, selfish ways of the world, which seem to bind us down so cruelly? We know that *love* is the way out, but we cannot follow the Law of Love if we have not faith enough to do so. If we desire to be delivered from the tyranny of life and the methods of the world, which crush the weak, giving the spoil to the strong, we must trust God to the extent that we rely entirely upon Him, at the same time ceasing to act harshly, ourselves, towards others.

Now, as we have already seen, faith can be developed in two ways:

1. Through experience, trial, test and difficulty. This is partly, although not wholly in all cases, involuntary.

2. Through experiment. This is wholly voluntary and through our own will and volition. That is to say, not only are we willing to trust God, but we actually do something which throws us entirely upon God, so that our faith is increased.

It would naturally be thought that by being boldly experimental one would develop faith entirely or, at any rate, partly, without the necessity of painful experience. It may be however, that it merely accelerates our progress, so that we learn rapidly through both processes. I think, although I am not sure about this, that one does avoid a great deal of suffering by being boldly experimental. In any case one benefits largely by experimenting in acts of faith and can lose nothing.

First, then, how is it possible to meet trouble and trial, adversity, and so on, in such a way as to turn them into blessings? How is it possible to deal with trouble in such a manner as will enable us to pass through it successfully?

Simply by keeping our thoughts up.

By refusing to be hypnotised by our troubles and seeming evil, and by staying our mind and thoughts upon God, we allow the Divine Order to appear. Divine Order is the reality. It is, in an inner sense, the natural order: all disorder being a distortion of life. When we raise our thoughts to the *ideal world and its designer*, and keep them there, ignoring as far as possible the disorder and seeming evil that are attacking us, we open ourselves and our life so that Divine Order can manifest.

By raising our thoughts to the inner perfection, which is the reality, or, in an inner sense, *natural order*, our mind becomes attuned to the Divine or Master Mind. After this it is only a question of time, for Divine Order must manifest outwardly sooner or later. So, we see that the greater our trouble the more completely our mind becomes stayed upon God, consequently the trouble is turned into a blessing, for we become changed into the likeness of THAT upon which we meditate.

But, you will say: "*How* can I raise my thoughts in this way, staying them upon God or the ideal perfection?" Now this is quite easy to one who has been practising thought-control for some years. Instantly, and without any effort, he can raise his thoughts to the ideal and real, turning away completely from time, sense, and sense-perception. He can also "stay" his mind upon God, on the ideal world, or the reality, as long as he pleases. But this is the result of years of patient, persevering practice. Therefore, those who are not as far advanced as this do not find it by any means easy.

The advanced worker just turns to God and can then "stay" his mind and attention upon the infinite and eternal. He does not have to make use of any words or affirmations. He simply turns to God as one friend does to another. Just as easily and just as naturally.

But with those less advanced it is a different story. The mind, thought, and attention simply cannot find God, or reality, or an ideal world upon which to become stayed or focused.

In order to become an adept in thought control it is necessary to set apart a certain time each day in a place where one will not be disturbed. By sitting quietly and by saying to oneself "I no longer think of outside things but stay my attention on the infinite and eternal", one becomes quiet, composed and detached from external things.

Next it may help to argue with oneself after this fashion: "Behind all change and decay is the Eternal and Infinite. All around me is the immanent presence of the Supreme Being. In this spiritual presence there is no evil, imperfection or disorder, but only divine good, perfection and order. On this my mind is fixed, in this my soul finds rest. In the peace of the Infinite, I find peace. Through contemplating Divine Order my whole life becomes ordered, peaceful and secure.

In the Divine Order there is no evil, imperfection, ugliness, disorder, weakness, confusion, or unrest, but only pure and holy good, perfection, beauty, order, peace, rest and satisfaction. In this divine spiritual presence, which is real and eternal, there is life, health, wholeness and power. As I contemplate these, they flow into me, regenerating me, making me a new creature after the Divine Image".

By denying that imperfection or disorder forms any part of the real or spiritual world or presence in which we live and move and have our being, and by affirming that in this presence or inner world of the spirit (the perfect expression of the divine idea) there is perfect order, wholeness, perfection, harmony, and peace, we gradually enter into a realisation of the truth of that which we affirm. Such denials and affirmations are statements of pure, unalloyed truth about the real and eternal; therefore, by making use of them, the mind becomes cleansed of error and filled with truth.

For a few years it may be necessary to make use of such statements of truth, but after that you will reach a state of realisation in which you will live perpetually, without effort.

By keeping the thoughts up, staying them upon the eternal, in this way, you will find that all trouble and difficulty will be overcome. Through keeping your thoughts stayed upon God and truth, the power of the Infinite will not only support you, but will also adjust your life, bringing everything into a state of harmony and peace. It may take time and may need patience and perseverance, but the final result is a foregone conclusion. It MUST and WILL come to pass.

Here, we believe, is the essential difference between our teaching and that of many others. The great secret is not to pray for certain things, or to be delivered from certain troubles, or for certain things to come to pass, but simply to keep our thoughts up, stayed up on the eternal, and to allow life to have its way with us. If we do this the only result can be harmony and peace; for we allow the Infinite to express its Perfect Plan through us. If, however, we pray, demand, or work mentally for certain things to become ours, or for our life to be altered in a certain way, or that other people should do certain things or not do certain other things; if we do this, we increase our difficulties immeasurably and create disorder and trouble of an acute kind.

Some students may not be ready to accept this teaching. They may not be ready to let life have its way with them. They may still want to have their own way, and to "work" for it. If so, they must go their own way and learn by experience the truth of what I have taught in this lesson and others.

Now, secondly, our faith can be increased by daring experiment. We can test God in the same way that one who is learning to swim must test or prove the buoyancy of water by trusting himself to it. Like the would-be swimmer, who has to throw himself on the water, allowing it to support him, so also do we have to cast ourselves upon God. We cast ourselves upon God by doing things which test our faith to the utmost. This does not mean doing foolish things exactly, although your action may appear to be foolish to those who are purely selfish and worldly-minded. It may to a businessman or woman be a great test of faith to refuse to take advantage of a favourable opportunity, which, however, does not square with his or her highest ideals. It may be a great trial of faith for one engaged in spiritual work to refuse to make use of worldly methods of raising money, and to trust the Spirit instead. It may be a great trial of faith to undertake a certain care or responsibility which may appear to be beyond you, yet which seems to be your duty. It is always a test of faith to do that which is right from a spiritual point of view, when expediency pulls very hard the other way.

The greatest test of faith is when we pray, "Thy Will be done", or "Lead Thou me on". We then cast ourselves out onto the deep. Self always wants to direct matters. It likes the help of God so as to do what it desires more effectively or easily, but it will not surrender to the Will of the Supreme. At some time or other we must all launch out into the deep, and this is at once the greatest act of faith and the greatest test of God. This does not mean that God can pass through a test, but that we prove God by trusting Him, completely and utterly.

We are so fearful and faithless when it comes to trusting our all to God. We are so afraid to trust One who is Infinite Love and Wisdom, and who desires for us only our highest good.

It is by launching out into the deep that our faith is built up. It is through trusting God experimentally that our faith grows from a tiny plant into a mighty tree.

And when we have launched out into the deep, what then? What we have to do is to go forward courageously and **Keep our thoughts up.**

At every step experiences will be met which will cause doubt and misgiving to arise. These should be met by short statements of truth such as:

HENRY THOMAS HAMBLIN

God is my help.
God is my deliverer.

Keep on, dear student, keep on. There are infinite glories ahead. I see before you the Dawn of a New Day, a day of surpassing beauty and blessedness, the rising of a sun that will never set.

Chapter Eight

Overcoming Temptation

Temptation is so cunning and masterly that it is no wonder we are deceived and easily led astray. When we first start out on the Path of the New Life we are filled with joy and exaltation; and temptation seems so far away that we are liable to fall into the error of thinking that it is a little thing, or that we are so changed that we can never be tempted to sin in the old way again. Thus, we are lulled into a sense of false security.

After a time, however, we are afflicted "full and sore". Then it is only by the power of omnipotence that we can be delivered and made conquerors.

Now you may wonder why you are tempted and tried to such an alarming extent. You may wonder why, even in your holiest moments, you may be tempted to do things which ordinary people who are not in the path would not think of doing.

The reason is this: all those who set out on the path of New Life have to pass through a whole series of experiences, often very trying, which gradually change them until they become entirely new creatures. The effect of all these experiences is to break down the old nature by degrees, and to build up in its place a new spiritual nature after the pattern of Jesus Christ.

We are continually tried and tempted on our weak points, and through overcoming they are made our strongest points. This process goes on until we become perfected. This is looking a long way ahead, but it is the object that we have in view. "Be perfect even as your Father in Heaven is perfect". Jesus did not utter these extraordinary words lightly: He meant them.

First, there are the temptations of the flesh or lower nature - the appetites, desires and lusts of the carnal nature - these are very trying to some students, but not to others. In some they are primitive, in others refined. In the former they are sensual; in the latter they are sensuous. They are both alike really, because they are only different expressions of the desire for gratification or satisfaction through sensation.

One by one these are dropped, naturally and gladly, until all such desires are transmuted.

Temptation then changes, becoming much more subtle, cunning and refined. The great and final enemy to be subdued is "the self". Self-interest continually insinuates itself into our holiest aims. It is "the self" that keeps us in the wilderness of separateness. Spiritual pride, the most fatal of all the sins, is based entirely on "self". One who has attained is entirely free from spiritual pride, simply because he has slain "the self" and has found the Universal Self.

Again, the temptation to have, to grasp, to possess, for the self, is very strong, subtle and most cunning. It may take several years to overcome. When, however, we overcome, and have passed through this phase of experience, we enter into liberty and freedom. Long after all desire for personal gain has passed there still remains the desire for praise, people's good opinion, popularity, etc. But all this is overcome in course of time, until our life becomes universal, so that we live for "self" no longer.

I do not think that indulging in a lot of retrospection is good for one. Examining one's motives may be all right, to a certain extent, but it is harmful if indulged in to any serious degree. My experience is that it is far better to keep the eyes fixed on God and eternal things, raising the thoughts to our highest conception of Good and Truth. If we do this then what is hindering us is revealed to us. Then we remove the barriers to the inflow of God's perfect life in us, by surrendering more fully to the operation of the Divine Will through all our being.

Now, you will ask, how can temptation be overcome? How can you be victorious both now and finally?

Not by fighting temptation in the ordinary sense of the term. This is the way of failure.

The whole secret is **attention.**

When we "fight" temptation, or the Devil, or whatever we may term it, we direct attention to it or him. Now "life" (the stream of life) flows in the direction of the attention. That is to say, if we direct the attention to a certain sin or indulgence, the forces of life flow in that direction, thus increasing the trouble. Here is an illustration. If we suffer from insomnia then the more we think about it and try to overcome it - in other words, fight it - the worse the trouble becomes. Whereas if we can forget it entirely, we sleep soundly. It is the same with temptation: by directing the attention to it we increase it. And this increase is cumulative.

On the other hand, it is certainly true that we must not weakly or thoughtlessly give in to temptation. We have to become sinless, and more than this, perfect. We are taught to resist the Devil, but to resist not evil. This seeming paradox will be explained next.

It is hardly necessary to emphasise this point here, but it is perhaps as well to remind ourselves that our final goal is faultless sinlessness. Nothing short of this will do. The real, inner object of temptation is to change us into perfect children of God, joint heirs with our older brother Jesus Christ, and friends of God.

How then, you will ask, can temptation be overcome? We have been told, probably from our youth up: "resist the Devil, and he will fly from you". It all depends upon *how* we resist. First, let me say, it is far better to resist in a wrong way and to fail, than not to resist at all. The old teaching that those who die fighting for truth, purity, sinlessness, etc., even though they fail, are saved, is perfectly sound. But how much better is it for us to overcome!

The paradox that we resist not evil and yet have to resist the Devil, the cause of evil, will now be explained.

The command to resist not evil refers to the experiences of life which we call evil but does not refer to temptation. It refers to persecution principally. No disciple in the Path ever resists persecution. It is part of the perfecting process and is so valuable that Jesus said that we should rejoice and be exceeding glad when we are called upon to endure it. It also refers to the so-called evil experiences of life, of its apparent injustices, etc. All these must be met with non-resistance, for this leads to liberty and freedom. Therefore, whatever other people may do to us, no matter how they may ill-treat us or try us, we must not resist, even in thought, but must forgive them and hold them in thoughts of good will.

But when we come to the subject of temptation it is quite another matter. Temptation really comes from within. If another person tempts us, it is because there is something in us which has attracted him or her. What takes place is really a warfare in our own hearts between good and evil, light and darkness, the higher and lower natures, our real Self and the self.

Now this lower nature that would drag us down, and its temptations, must be resisted, but how? Just fighting it only increases the trouble, for it directs the attention to it, so that impulse and desire become stronger.

The lower must be transmuted into the higher.

This cannot be accomplished by directing the attention to the temptation, but by directing the whole of our attention upwards, to God, to a power greater than our own, greater than our lower nature, our desires, lusts, appetites, selfishness, love of the self, etc.: greater than the Devil, or Lucifer, or whatever we may term the subtle forces which seek to drag us down: to the one omnipotent power. Now there is only one omnipotent power, otherwise it would not be omnipotent. When we turn to God there is no other power at all; therefore, we become free, immediately.

We are in bondage and subject to lower powers, so long as we do not turn to God. But immediately we turn to God, the omnipotent power, good and perfection, we become free, in and through His omnipotence, for all other powers cease to be. Ponder over this statement, for it contains one of the greatest arcane truths, which, when apprehended by the soul, through spiritual illumination, lifts one into freedom.

Now, what do I mean by turning to God? I mean directing the attention to a power, intelligence, wisdom, and love, far greater than my own; to a being who is ever above, beyond, transcendent, so wonderful in power, wisdom and love is He, yet who is also closer to us than breathing. We accomplish this through the top of the head.

As we direct the attention literally upwards, we rise above the physical and psychic, making contact with the spiritual. It is as though above our head is a funnel through which the divine, superconscious, eternal life flow.

Each student must follow the method that seems most suitable to him or her, but personally I find it best to close the eyes and then to turn them upwards in their sockets, as though trying to see something immediately above my head. Some students who are more psychically or spiritually sighted than I, state that they see immediately above them a beautiful being, or Angel, or Christ, who leads them out of danger into harmony and peace, and who lifts them above the power of temptation. Be this as it may, the fact remains that by directing the attention upwards in this way, Divine Life and power flow into us, making us entirely new creatures.

Now the secret of overcoming is an entire surrender to, and trust in, the Higher Power or Christ (i.e. that which is above us). None of self, but all of Thee, must be our constant prayer. We have to acknowledge that of ourselves we are helpless and an easy prey to temptation; and we have to put our trust entirely in the ONE above us. So long as we put our trust in self, thinking that we can conquer, we are helpless and at the mercy of every harmful influence. If, however, we concentrate our attention upon the near presence, or Centre of Power, just above us, saying: "Thou alone canst deliver: Thou alone canst save: I put my trust in Thee": if we do this, then temptation can have no power over us at all.

But this turning upwards, to a power greater than our own power must be done early. There must be no temporising with the enemy. The temptation is not suggested to us openly in all its native ugliness, but first there is suggested a thought which may not appear to be so very bad or dangerous in itself, but which if accepted or "played with" leads on to the real temptation. By "played with" I mean allowed to have our attention even for a moment. As soon as we allow the thought to claim our attention or interest, our first defence is broken down, and after that it is almost impossible not to give way to the temptation proper. It is in these early stages that the attention must be turned immediately to the greater power present with us, with the thought or prayer: "None of self but all of Thee", which is an acknowledgement that of ourselves we can do nothing, but that the power of God is the only one that can deliver us, and that we are, here and now, saved, preserved and delivered.

Another most important thing is this: if we fail, we must not think anything about it, but simply pick ourselves up, and, keeping our attention fixed on the ONE above us, forgetting all about our fall. If we think about our fall, we direct attention to it, which is simply the very thing that must be avoided at all costs. *Confess your shortcomings only once, and then think of them no more, for they are all forgiven and forgotten* by God, so why should *you* remember them! The great thing is to keep the attention up through the top of the head to the higher plane, or Being, where all power and help are instantly available

Chapter Nine

Overcoming Habit

We continually suffer through our bad habits, for they bring to us their fruits which are always painful and unpleasant. For instance, late rising not only robs a man of a "before breakfast" life of joy and inspiration, but it may undermine his health, keep him from rising in his calling, and may finally ruin him altogether. Rising late compels him to eat hurriedly and rush off to his occupation, only to arrive in an unfit state for his work. This makes him less efficient than he would otherwise be, and therefore less successful, while his hurried eating may ruin his digestion, thus leading to a complete breakdown in health and loss of employment, business or position.

Thus, we see how much suffering comes through such a comparatively small bad habit as late rising. This bad habit, of course, is due to a weakness of character. One who cannot rise at the time he should, lacks willpower, self-control and power to act. It does not always indicate sloth on the part of a man, for some who rise late are industrious and are willing to work late, but it shows that he is a slave to habit, and that his character is too weak to overcome it.

Now, in this lesson I do not deal with specific habits, but only with habit generally. Then you will be able to apply it according to your need. There is no one, I think, who does not possess some weakness of character, or who does not suffer from some habit which he would like to break.

Some, of course, would give all they possess in order to be free.

Habit may not in the first place be due to weakness of character, for one is liable to drift into a habit unconsciously almost, but inability to break the habit shows that the victim is a slave. This state of affairs need not remain. The most terrible of bad habits, that may have enslaved a person for the best part of a lifetime, can be broken, and the victim set entirely free. In the doing of it the character is built up. The two processes go on concurrently, and the final result is a free man or woman, and a fine, strong character.

Overcoming habit, or breaking its power and emerging into liberty, is much the same as resisting temptation. It cannot be accomplished in our own power - that is the power of the personal will or finite self - but only in the power of the Infinite. The power of a long-established bad habit is so great that it is only the power of omnipotence that can deal with it successfully. By the term "bad habit" I mean any habit that is out of our control. Sometimes the so-called small or unimportant habits are the worst and most difficult to eradicate.

Like temptation, the repetition of a habit begins with thought. If we fall it is due to our having entertained the thought or suggestion of it. A physical craving there may be, but this suggests a thought of indulging it. We may not be able to control the craving, but we can deal with the thought. If the latter is dealt with in the right manner, then the craving is overcome. For instance, there may be a craving for alcohol, but this produces the thought or suggestion that we should go and have a drink. We cannot prevent the craving, but we can deal with the thought or suggestion. Every time the thought or suggestion is successfully dealt with, the craving is reduced in intensity. Every time that we overcome in this way, we make it easier to overcome next time. The results are cumulative, and this is one way by which "God helps those who help themselves."

For years I have made a close study of the subject of habit as it affects me personally. In every case I have found that failure has been due to entertaining a forbidden thought. If we trace the whole regrettable incident back to its source, we find that, in the earliest stage of all, there has been the admittance of a thought. Right back in the far distance, so to speak, is a door through which every thought or suggestion has to enter. If the thought or suggestion is not admitted then the temptation to repeat a habit, or to fall back into a habit, cannot occur. If, however, the thought or suggestion is allowed to enter, then, in spite of our utmost efforts of resistance, we are liable to fall.

Resisting temptation is like maintaining a dam. There can be no danger of the dam collapsing so long as the first little leak is attended to. It is then quite an easy matter to stop the trouble. If, however, a small leak is neglected then the utmost exertions of all the inhabitants are incapable of preventing disaster.

How, then, are we to deal with temptation in its earliest stage? Armed with the knowledge that the battle is decided at the gate, where the thought or suggestion has to find entrance, we say: "No, I will not accept this thought, therefore the incident is closed". This may be wonderfully effective, for a time, and even for a long time. We may even pat ourselves on the back and congratulate ourselves upon the fact that we are free. Nothing is more fatal than such self-congratulation. It weakens our defences: it lulls us to sleep, it makes possible a successful onslaught of the enemy, and then, before we are aware of it, he is in, and the fortress has fallen.

It is possible, however, by sheer thought control, in the earliest stage, to go on for years successfully. But then, when we think that the enemy is dead, we are subjected to an onslaught so severe and so cleverly subtle, that we may find ourselves overwhelmed. Great is our alarm and consternation to find all at once that the old devil is not dead at all, but apparently stronger than ever.

All, however, is not lost, or need not be. We must not think that it is no use trying anymore. This is just what "the other side" would like us to think. The whole experience is part of our training. It is only through being taught, through bitter failure and experience, our utter dependence upon God, that we can become what we are destined to be. We have to become God-men or God-women: that is, we have to let the power of the Infinite work through us; with the result that we become new creatures, created anew through the Infinite Power that we "allow" to flow through us.

Now the first step towards this wonderful consummation is that we realise completely and fully that we of ourselves cannot conquer, and that it must be God's power working through us that must overcome. So long as we think that we, our finite selves, can overcome, we are bound to fall sooner or later. We have to acknowledge that God, or a Higher Power, the Power of the Spirit, and not our finite self-power, is the only way by which temptation can be overcome. Through this acknowledgment we surrender to this Higher Power, and it is through such surrender that we make it possible for the Power of the Spirit to flow through us and overcome for us. When our will thus becomes, through surrender, at-one with the will of the Highest, then what was impossible before becomes possible.

But there must not only be this surrender and acknowledgement in a general sense, it must also be made use of in a certain way. We have to get right back to the little gate through which the first thought or suggestion has to enter and there make this acknowledgement. If this is done, then the door cannot open to the destructive thought or suggestion. As soon as the temptation thought attempts to enter, we must turn to God or a Higher Power than our own, saying: "Not of myself but only through Thee," or similar words. Whatever the words used may be, they should be an acknowledgment that we are helpless without God, and at the same time, an invocation of the power of God on our behalf.

This could be expressed very perfectly and thoroughly in a long sentence, but what is needed is something short and sharp. There is no time to dally, the remedy must be applied **at once**; otherwise, the enemy will capture our attention, after which our citadel is in danger of falling. What has to be said must be said quickly, immediately, and there is no time either to think of, or repeat, a long sentence. Like lightning the attention must be directed to God or a Higher Power before it can be captured from the enemy, and this can be accomplished by a quick short statement. One that I have used successfully has been: Only Thee, and also another: None of self but all of Thee. Of course, it is done mentally and not audibly and therefore is done very quickly.

Now when tempted in some ways, a certain amount of nervous energy is aroused, which seeks to be exploded in the form of the particular indulgence to which we are subject. For instance, if our failing is a bad temper there is a tremendous amount of nervous energy aroused and generated, which is exploded as soon as something irritates us. Now if we suppress an outburst of temper, we injure our health. If we allow it to vent itself on others, we injure them. The only thing to do is to guide the energy into a different channel. Say to yourself: "I will now use this energy in doing this work." Then set to work on something useful and work the energy off on that. Thus, instead of hurting either yourself or other people, you do something useful and constructive. Also, you help to cure yourself of a bad habit.

There is also another way by which a little common sense can help, which is that: if temptation comes to you while you are idle, immediately reverse the thoughts as already taught in this lesson, and then get up and DO something, preferably something useful. As you have already been taught the great thing is to divert the attention from the suggestion or thought that is attacking you. Getting on the move, putting yourself in the care of the Higher Power, and then doing something that will engage and occupy the attention will accomplish this effectively. But there must be no parleying, no hesitating. Instant action is necessary. It is a well-known fact that some people when giving up drinking or smoking find it helpful to suck a sweet or eat an apple when the craving comes on. Doing so diverts the attention, and it is because of this, rather than the pleasure of eating the sweet or apple, which makes the practice helpful.

But in spite of all our efforts it may be that we come to the end of our tether, humbled by failure, and brought to the very verge of despair. Then it is that we have to acknowledge, with a completeness and abandon such as we have never expressed before, that we cannot do anything right, and that if we are to be delivered then God must do it and do it in His own way. It is often at this time, when this surrender is made, that the tide turns, and we then find that the habit is dying away.

This is a tremendous task, the overcoming of habit. It may engage our most earnest, not to say desperate, attention, off and on, for years. But if we keep looking up and doing our best according to the teaching of this Lesson, deliverance must surely come.

Summary:

In order to overcome temptation, we have to

1. Keep out the first thought of suggestion.

2. At the *first* assault of the small gate we must turn at once to God or a Higher Power, acknowledging our own weakness and invoking the aid of *omnipotence*. This can be helped by the use of a very short sentence such as: "Not of myself, but only Thee".

3. Energy aroused by temptation must be diverted into another channel in the form of work. By this means grave diseases are avoided.

4. If tempted when at rest or in idleness, immediately get up and DO something, so as to arouse interest in another subject, and also to use up or work off the energy aroused.

Finally...

Do not, on any account, either boast (save in Christ and not in yourself) or congratulate yourself. We are tempted to do this when we find ourselves apparently free from a habit or besetting sin. If we fall into this error, we find that the habit or besetting sin is not dead at all. This applies to other departments of life. If we say: "Oh,

I NEVER catch a cold," we are likely to get a bad one immediately. Instead of boasting let us put our whole trust in God.

Chapter Ten

Overcoming Adversity and Trouble

Times of adversity are due partly to the ebb and flow of life generally, and partly to attraction. All through life and nature we see contrast. It is said that it is only through this that we can appreciate anything at all. There is light and darkness, summer and winter, heat and cold, the beautiful and the ugly, and so on, ad infinitum, almost. In the same way, there are joyful and sunny times in life, and there are also sorrowful and wintry periods as well. Both are trying: both are a test.

Of the two, times of happiness and ease are by far the more dangerous to the soul.

Then there is also attraction. We attract to ourselves those experiences which purify the soul. Now, it is well known to all Christian Mystics that there is nothing more efficacious than loss, grief and trouble. They not only purify, but they also induce humbleness, without which it is impossible to approach God, or make progress in the spiritual life. All these experiences generally come together, so that before we are well through one trouble another appears. These together form a period of adversity. At such times we are conscious that things are not working WITH us, and that there are influences working AGAINST us.

It is, therefore, not due to any evil influence that troubles all come together, winter is just as necessary as summer in the natural world; and wintry times in our life and experience are just as necessary as times of prosperity and expansion. The one is as good as the other.

But we are not mere puppets in the hands of fate. Much depends upon how we meet our troubles and times of adversity. For instance, given an adverse period of certain length and severity, entirely different results might accrue from it, in the case of two men passing through this adverse period.

If a man blunders into such a period without knowledge or preparation, consequently meeting his experiences in the wrong way, and in the wrong spirit, he multiplies his troubles and difficulties. But if, on the other hand, he meets life's adverse periods steadfastly, co-operatively and willingly, he comes through them victoriously, all the better for the experience.

The great fact that we have to face is that during times of adversity we meet with trouble, it may be grief, sorrow, loss, faithlessness, desertion, disappointment, to a greater or less degree. Why we meet with these things need not concern us very much, the great thing is

How we should act during such periods

Now, first of all as regards a period of adversity. Let us realise that it is a period, or spell, during which the chill winds of life's experiences blow up on us. Otherwise, we may spend quite a lot of time and energy in a misplaced effort to understand why everything goes wrong with us, why we meet with all this trouble while others enjoy lives of untroubled happiness, what or where we have gone wrong in our study and application of truth, etc. It is useless and unprofitable for us to think along these lines. It may also be harmful, for it may lead to worry. We may worry because we fear that things have gone wrong permanently: that God has forsaken us; that we have taken the wrong turning, etc. None of these is true. The truth is that we have entered a wintry period, just as in March (in England) we enter a period of east winds. The east wind keeps on blowing, day after day, and it is most searching and uncomfortable, but we do not mind much, because we know that it is only for a few weeks, after which the south and westerly breezes will bring relief and comfort. It is just the same with periods of adversity in our life: they come, and they go, to be replaced in due course by times of spiritual refreshment and peace.

Now let us carry this analogy of the east wind and times of adversity a little farther. Let us consider what a lot depends upon how we meet a period of easterly winds. We have to meet such a period differently from the way we meet a period of summer weather. In summer we get thoroughly hot with exercise and then throw ourselves down on the ground for the wind to cool us. But it would not be wise to do this in March when the east wind chills, searches and finds out our weak spots. Instead, we put up our defences by wearing adequate clothing, keeping on the move in order to stimulate the circulation, and, in addition, maintaining a positive attitude of mind, which is the reverse of fear, and yet is the antithesis of boasting or bravado. In other words, we act differently in March (in England) to what we do in July.

Now let us apply this to the subject we have in hand. When times of adversity come upon us, we must act differently from the way we act when enjoying prosperous and easy times. Times of adversity are not times suitable for the launching of ambitious schemes, or for risking our all in speculative ventures. The temptation, when an adverse period is entered upon, and we find things going wrong, is to become wild and frantic, trying to retrieve our fortunes by engaging in greater and more hazardous risks. The more things go wrong, the more we try, vainly, alas, to push things along. I knew a man once who lost a very fine business, and the whole of his capital, running into many thousands of pounds, and also all his property, simply through giving way to this tendency. He launched out into greater expenditure in order to increase his dwindling business, but all in vain. If he had cut down his expenses and "marked time" until the adverse period had passed, he would have been a prosperous man today.

It is hard to launch a boat on a shallow beach, when the tide is running out quickly. No sooner have you got partly clear than you get aground somewhere else. Then, after frantic efforts to race the receding tide, you may get clear only to find that the tide has fallen so much you can never reach the open water. But how different is it on a rising tide! No frantic efforts are required, but all that you need do is to wait until the boat is lifted off the mud or shingle, after which you can go wherever you desire.

Once, years ago at Eastbourne, when a westerly gale was blowing, I noticed quite a number of tramp steamers anchored near shore. I asked a friendly waterman why they did so, because being steamers they could have got round Beachy Head in spite of the wind. Then it was explained to me that both wind and tide were against the vessels, therefore it was cheaper to wait until conditions were more favourable. By waiting for a favourable tide and a less violent wind they would save greatly, both in fuel and wear and tear.

It is just the same with life. It pays to wait and to husband our strength and our resources, when an adverse period has to be traversed. We need to go slowly and to be watchful and careful, in one sense: though in another sense, we are careful (anxious) about nothing, because we know that the Spirit of Truth will see us safely through, and that all we have to do is to be patient, faithful, and to keep our thoughts in Heavenly places.

Now this advice may seem to be very worldly and materially minded. It may be, but it is valuable, nevertheless. Also, where the material life ends, and the spiritual begins no one can say. Indeed, if we are led by the Spirit in all our affairs, then the whole of our life becomes spiritual, and all our experiences, no matter how mundane they may appear to be, are spiritual experiences. Thus, such prosaic things as paying rent, rates and taxes, moving to a fresh town, entering new work, dealing with difficult people, and, last but not least, the humdrum routine of life, "the mud and scum of things", all these, become spiritual events, used, every one of them, by the Spirit, in our re-education.

Consequently, we say no longer, "What is the use of all this drudgery?" for we know that it forms part of our spiritual training.

Thus, in dealing with mundane affairs we are being exercised in spiritual disciplines. By bringing the Spirit into all our activities, every department of our life becomes spiritualized.

I have already said that what we have to do, during times of adversity, is to wait and be patient. There is probably nothing more difficult. Yet the fact that everything that we do, and every new venture ends in disaster, should warn us that the times are not propitious for a step forward. If we are being led by the Spirit, that is, if we have committed all our ways and affairs to God, desiring only that Infinite Wisdom should guide us, then there are signs by which we may know the way.

The way of the Spirit is one of harmony and peace. It is not one of strife, friction, upset, unpleasantness, difficulty, or of failure. In the Spirit everything is in its right place, at the right time. If we find that everything is out of place, that the time is all wrong, and that all is friction and discord, we may know that the Spirit has nothing to do with it. What I mean by the time being wrong is this. Just like the timing of an engine which ensures that every operation of its various parts is performed always exactly at the right moment and fraction of a moment, so is the way of the Spirit. Everything is timed perfectly. Just the right thing comes, just at the right moment; or the necessary opening is made, just when we are ready for it, and so on. In the Spirit everything works together like a well-oiled and perfectly timed machine: nothing is late, and nothing is too early.

Now, if an engine is wrongly "timed", so that its valves do not move exactly at the right moment, then either it will not work at all, or if it does perform, it can do so only inefficiently, and with great difficulty and labour. It is the same with life. If all our ventures and undertakings are discordant and out of joint, full of difficulty and friction, then we may be sure that we are not working with the Spirit, and that the path we are mapping out, or trying to follow, is not that of the Spirit.

Of course, I do not mean that we are not to overcome the ordinary difficulties of life. We have to be men and women of action, decision, courage, perseverance and application. But those who are spiritually awake can develop a sense of intuitional awareness and sensitiveness, by means of which they can tell when the Spirit is with them and when it is not. The watchword to remember is: **The way of the Spirit is harmony and peace.**

But times of adversity are not to be overcome only by waiting until the Spirit has prepared the way. We overcome also by raising our thoughts above our troubles. Thus, when we are stricken by grief and bereavement, we must rise above them and praise God for all His love and mercy. Grief, if "indulged in", or given into, becomes a curse, for it is then the forerunner of many other ills. If, however, we rise above it, praising God for His love and mercy, wisdom and over-ruling all things for good, we become raised to a higher vibration, so that no other negative ill is attracted. Also, what is far more important, our spiritual life becomes stimulated and encouraged, our character is enriched and developed, and we are immeasurably blessed through an experience, which, if we had given into it, would have been a curse and a destructive influence, blighting the whole of the life.

This is the way to a life of victory and overcoming, also to the acquirement of a degree of positive mindedness such as nothing else can achieve. It leads also to calmness of spirit in any circumstances, and also to steadfastness of mind; for praise brings us into the realm of certainty, wherein we know, instead of merely indulging in hopes.

If we sit down, for five minutes only, praising and blessing God with our whole heart, or even merely repeating such words as: **praise, blessing, overcoming, victory, joy,** we become braced up and quite new creatures by the time we have finished. This is due to a true, positive state or condition, or higher vibration being wrought in us through true prayer.

If we are so constituted that we can only repeat the words just given, it is good; but it is better, if we can, to use more of a prayer, such as: "I thank Thee, I praise Thee, I adore Thee". As we keep repeating these words it is as though we were lifted up out of a stifling, confining, impeding, morass, into liberty, light and freedom. Then as we are lifted up, we can feel new life and power quickening us. And this way the state of stifling, deadening, destroying depression and negativeness, if given into, would almost destroy us, or at best would greatly spoil our life, is overcome. The great secret is this, that the important thing is not that our life should be changed, but that we should be lifted right out of the numbing, deadening depression and negativeness, into liberty and freedom. After that the outer life becomes adjusted, just at the right time and in the right way. In other words, it is not our circumstances that have to be altered, but we ourselves have to be changed. As we become raised, through praise and thanksgiving, so do we become changed. As we are raised up, new life flows into us - it is the Inner Life of God, that mysterious eternal life of which the Apostles speak, as of something rare and difficult of attainment. Praise is the OPEN SESAME.

The life of praise is the life of power.

Chapter Eleven

Unity and Oneness

Divine guidance and protection

When we enter into unity with Christ, the Lord of Love, becoming one with the Eternal, all fear is cast out, we become Divinely guided, and we are Divinely protected.

All our troubles are due to separateness - all our fears, all our liability to become lost and to meet with what are called evil happenings. Be it noted that I do not speak as one who has attained to this perfect state; but, rather, as one who follows afar off, breathless but pursuing. I know the path and am anxious to show it to others, but I often fail myself. Nevertheless, I shall never cease pursuing, because of the hunger the Lord has put in my heart. Therefore, it is not a teacher who is speaking to you, but only a fellow pilgrim on the secret path of inner life or regeneration.

The Path, though arcane, is yet very simple; but although very simple, it is not by any means easy. It is only by treading a difficult path that we can become fit for the Kingdom of Heaven. The teaching is not difficult to our understanding but is difficult to put into practice.

This is because it goes against the old nature to act according to the new, or Divine, nature.

The great gulf that separates us from the Divine is lack of love. We may possess faith that is so great it may remove mountains; we may give all our goods to feed the poor; we may possess the gift of prophecy and do mighty works, yet if we are not children of Divine love, expressing it in all our actions, thoughts, impulses and feelings, we are nothing, so St. Paul tells us, but empty sound, or a lifeless shell.

The main difficulty is that we are not yet perfect in love. When we are made perfect it is possible to enter into unity with the Divine; we can then become one with our Lord; we can become live branches of the true Vine, but not before. When this stage is reached all fear departs; and when all fear is banished no evil can affect us. Like Daniel, when put in the lion's den, and like Shadrach, Meshach and Abednego, when thrown into the furnace, no evil or danger can affect us. We are promised in holy writ that we shall be able to drink deadly poisons, and they shall not hurt us, and that no pestilence shall have any power over us. Again, let me say that I do not dare speak as one who has attained, but as one who follows afar off and who is often very much out of breath trying to keep up with it all. But knowledge and understanding come to us all by degrees, inwardly. We know these things to be true, even though we have not yet attained to them. I know, through inward conviction or understanding, that what we call miracles are just as simple and natural as anything that we call "natural" in the ordinary experiences of life. Why do I speak with authority, or dogmatically, although I cannot quote any learned writers, or profound books? Simply because of this inward knowing, which bids me speak thus, even though I have not yet myself attained. Miracles are just as easy and natural as the ordinary events of life to one who has attained, simply because he can work in a higher consciousness - a consciousness that transcends the ordinary consciousness of three dimensions, in which we naturally and ordinarily are imprisoned.

Now we must not be led away by too much talk on "Higher consciousness" and "Fourth Dimension" and things of this character. It is possible for us to become quite learned on these subjects, and yet to remain as far away from the Kingdom as ever. It is also possible to enter the Kingdom of God and yet to possess no head knowledge of these things. This is because true religion and real attainment are matters of the heart and practical living, rather than of the intellect and theory. It is through putting love into practice that entrance is won into the Kingdom, and not by theorising about it.

But here, again, we may fall into grievous error. Even the law of love may be used in a wrong way. It is possible to use this law, simply because we know that it is only by making use of currents of love and forgiveness that we can be protected from enemies and various evils. We may use it in this metaphysical way, in order to attain our own ends and to ensure our own comfort, and yet for real love never to have touched our hearts at all. Thus, here we have the startling paradox that by using the law of love it is possible to become more selfish and hard-hearted than before; that is by using it metaphysically. Many people have been driven away from metaphysical teachings through this hardness and lack of real love and sympathy.

To use the Law of Love in order to get results, and to love for Love's sake are two very different things. The former leads away from the Kingdom; the latter brings us into living union with the Divine.

So we see, then, that it is not by theoretical knowledge, neither is it by a metaphysical use of the Law of Love in order to obtain results, that we can find the Kingdom, but only through loving for Love's sake. First our hearts have to be touched by Divine Love, and our naturally selfish, hard nature melted; and then by loving all in a Divine way, in pity and compassion - not in order to benefit ourselves in any way, but only for Love's sake - in this way, and in this way alone, we are made fit for the Kingdom. When the soul is brought to judgement, claims to cleverness, metaphysical knowledge and ability to get "results" will be of no avail. Only Love, Divine Love, can stand the test of that great day.

It is possible also to go on for years studying, talking, and even writing about love, unity, oneness, etc., and to be quite learned about it, yet never to make any advance in the spiritual life. Love is not a thing to be talked about, it has to be expressed and radiated just where we are, amongst those with whom we are living and working.

Again, love is not a negative thing; it is not a mere abstention from harshness, unkindness, resentment, bitterness and retaliation. It is, of course, a step forward to abstain from these things, if hitherto we have indulged in them. But Divine Love - for it is Divine Love and not mere "creaturely" love that we have to express - is a live and radiant thing. It is giving out, a radiation of pity, compassion, sympathy, forgiveness, help, encouragement, and a *yearning* after the well-being of others. Divine love is born in us and is active in us, when we can yearn over humanity with a great yearning, crying out to God "with groanings which cannot be uttered": "Oh, that they might know what I know. Oh, that they might have the inward joy that possesses me. Oh, that they might know Thee, the only true God; whom to know is life eternal".

But words are limited in expression, and cannot convey the yearning of our heart, but they express some of it. If we pray for others with greater yearning than we pray for ourselves, then we can be sure that we are being led by the Holy Spirit into the bonds of unity and universal love. As our love becomes more universal and more yearning, we become more like Christ, who bore the burdens of all men and also their sorrows. "And the Lord hath laid on Him the iniquity of us all". The more we advance in the spiritual life the more we bear, willingly, the burden and sorrows of humanity. And the sorrow and yearning that comes upon us breaks down the old nature which hitherto has kept us separate from Christ and brings us daily into closer union and oneness with Him, and in unity with the Whole.

Now this unity and oneness through Divine Love working in us, casts out fear. When we realise that God is love itself, we have no more fear. We have then worked through the wrath and darkness, as Jacob Boehme would call it, and have come into the light and liberty of the Spirit. This is a long process and takes many years, but those who are steadfast make steady progress, so that each year finds us wonderfully changed.

When there is an entire absence of fear due to a consciousness of Divine Love and the Divine Presence, no evil can affect us. It literally shuts the mouths of lions. It is only if, or when, fear enters in that any harm can affect us. A missionary once told me that when he was faced by menacing crowds of armed natives, the Lord took away all his fear, and he went up to them calmly and comfortably, although they certainly meant to murder him. God took away the missionary's fear (and by so doing protected him) because he had entered into the unity of love. He loved God and he loved the natives. All this teaching is contained in the few simple words of our Lord: "Thou shalt love the Lord thy God with all thy heart, and with all thy soul, and with all thy mind ... and thou shalt love thy neighbour as thyself".

You may say that faith also is needed. Yes, but love engenders trust, and this is, I think, probably the highest form of faith. Faith seems to belong more to the intellect, but trust belongs to the heart and intuition. And it is by the heart and intuition that we find God and enter into fellowship with Him. "Except ye be converted and become as little children, ye shall not enter into the Kingdom of

Heaven", said Jesus. It is not only in humbleness that we have to become as children, but in trust also. If we trust God as a child trusts its parents, we can experience no fear. A very little boy once was out with his father. Presently he saw a herd of cattle approaching, and being timid, he ran back to his father, put his hand in his, and said: "The cows are coming". His trust in his father was perfect. He felt quite sure that he was safe so long as his hand was clasped in that of his father. Even if the cattle had been a herd of wild buffalo, he would have felt equally safe. Neither would his trust have been misplaced, for his father, because of his great love for his child, would willingly have laid down his life to protect him. This is the kind of trust that we need. This is why "perfect love casts out fear". When we realise that God's love to us is immeasurably greater than that of the best earthly father for his son, can we not trust Him even as a little boy did his father?

"Yes", some of us may say, "I know that all this is true, but I cannot feel it, I cannot realise this truth in my heart. It is only head knowledge at present". In reply to this, let me say that there is one royal, direct and happy way to a full and complete entrance into a realisation of the love of God, the love that passeth all understanding, but which, thank God, we can realise and in it find rest to our souls. This is very simple: it is simply thanking God. If we keep on raising our heart and mind to God, saying:

"I thank Thee for thy wonderful love"

and will persist in so doing, making it a settled habit, then gradually a realisation of the love of God, in all its wonder and immensity, dawns in our soul. Then is cast out all fear, all doubt. We know and realise what the love of God means and that is sufficient.

This is the secret of all attainment, which is as far as possessing the gifts of the Spirit is concerned. If we desire to be filled with the Holy Spirit (for God's glory and not our own), then if we thank God for the gift of the Holy Spirit, in course of time we become filled. We can pray:

"I thank Thee for the Holy Spirit which works in us, makes us new creatures, and fills us with Divine Life and Power".

This can be used in conjunction with the yearning prayer of the heart which can be continually breathed: "Come Lord of Life and Love into my heart", or "Come, Lord into my heart, I yield all to Thee". This is the way of Unity through Love.

Then quite naturally, being conscious of God's love, and being filled by His Spirit, we are guided, not only in all our affairs, but also into all truth. We not only wait upon God, but we "wait for the Lord" in all things. And then we find that the way of the Spirit is harmony and peace. We may have to do some reaping of the mistakes and wrong "sowing" of earlier days: but even in this the hand of Love is to be found, over-ruling all things for good, even our mistakes and sins. For our God is a God who restores and heals.

Chapter Twelve

Divine Union

God has created us for Himself that we might dwell with Him in unity and love. Consequently, our souls can find no rest until they find it in Him.

Whatever may be our views as to "the Fall" and the origin of man, we have to acknowledge that God's final purpose in our case has not yet been achieved. We are not yet dwelling in our Father's house in unity and love. Our individual views as to the cause of our present state do not matter very much in face of the great truth that God has created us for Himself, and although we are still outside, He is drawing us to Himself through love.

God has loved us all down the ages. His great plan all through, from "before time was", has been to draw us to Himself, *through love*. The consummation of all God's vast operations through time and space is simply union with Him in Christ, our Divine Lord. Therefore, God's wonderful plan that is being worked out through the ages, and great eons of time, narrows itself down to the union of the soul of man with the Divine. The great plan of the ages is that we should become sons and daughters of God, nothing less.

Our individual views as to the cause of man's present position may, however, vary, but this does not much matter. One great essential fact remains, which is, that in our natural state we are not fit for the Kingdom of Heaven. Before we can enter into union with the Divine, we have to be changed, utterly and completely. Of ourselves, we can do nothing in this respect, except to co-operate with the Spirit's dealings with us.

It is the work of the Holy Spirit entirely that we have become changed to the extent we have. At one time we have loved the things which we now hate and hated the things we now love. This is not due to any virtue in ourselves but is due entirely to the work of the Spirit. All that we have had to do has been to co-operate with this work, and keep up with it, so to speak.

The new birth took place in us when our desires became changed, and we loathed both ourselves and our mode of life, and began to long for the richer and purer, more exalted and satisfying life of the Spirit. Mystically speaking, then was the Christ child born in us, conceived by the Holy Ghost. The soul has to be impregnated with Divine Life before there can be born in us a new self, a Christ, or child of God.

And this Divine One in us grows and grows until:

> We all come in the unity of the faith, and of the knowledge of the Son of God, unto a perfect man,

unto the measure of the stature of the fullness of Christ.

Ephesians 4:13

We have to attain to the measure of the stature of Christ. We have to allow the Christ child, born in us, conceived of the Holy Ghost, to reach maturity, until self becomes swallowed up, or absorbed in Christ, so that Christ becomes all-in-all. Now it is because God's plan concerning us is what it is that made Jesus affirm again and again that what He had come to do was to fulfil the will of his Father: and, again, that "it is not everyone that saith unto me Lord, Lord, who shall enter the Kingdom of Heaven; but he that doeth the will of My Father which is in Heaven". Again, our Lord said: "And everyone that heareth these sayings of mine and doeth them (that is, doeth the Will of my Father in Heaven) I will liken him unto a wise man who built his house upon a rock. And the rain descended, and the floods came, and the winds blew, and beat upon that house; and it fell not: for it was founded upon a rock".

Now the will of God is that we should become new creatures, through a new birth; through growth of the inward, spiritual life; through regeneration. We might, of course, talk about these things until "the crack of doom" without being a bit the wiser, better or richer for it. Talk and head knowledge will not carry us forward an inch, but only living the life and passing through the various experiences connected with the new regenerative life. Doing the will of "My Father which is in Heaven" means, principally, passing through all the various experiences connected with the several stages of regeneration, co-operatively and willingly. As we continually raise our thoughts and heart God-wards, not only does the regenerative life of the Holy Spirit flow into us, doing a wonderful work in us, gradually changing us into the likeness of "the Son", but also experiences are attracted to us which help us in our spiritual journey, in that they break down the "old man" and build up the new nature after the Divine pattern in Christ Jesus.

Princess Karadja, a great mystical writer, says that the stages of regeneration are as follows:

1. Repentance and the New Birth.

2. Interior Illumination.

3. Divine Communion.

4. Penance, or the Ordeal of Inner Judgement.

5. The complete Yielding up of the will to God.

6. Sanctification, when we are made Kings and Priests unto God (Rev. 1-6) having been perfected.

7. Union of the Soul with its Lord.[1]

Whatever stage we may be at, however, does not alter the fact the final goal is a life of complete faith and love. I find that all

---

1. Karadja, Princess Mary, died ca. 1935.

the experiences that are crowding upon me now are building up my faith, deepening my trust in God, and increasing my love and sympathy to all. I realise, as never before, that the path is so narrow that to follow it is like being balanced on a knife edge, and it is only by continually calling upon God and trusting Him entirely, that I can be sustained and brought safely through. What is true in my case will doubtless be true of all, because the way of attainment is the same for all, except as regards detail. We need not worry or think too much about the various stages of regeneration or spiritual growth, because God, the Holy Spirit, has our unfoldment in hand, and if we unreservedly put our trust in Him, then everything takes place at the right time, so that the necessary changes in us all come to pass in their right order, according to Divine plan directed by infinite wisdom.

Whatever we may claim or aspire to in spiritual attainment brings to us a series of experiences either to test our claim, or to prepare us for that to which we aspire. Unless we know this, we are apt to be either discouraged or non-plussed by what happens. Writers on spiritual subjects notice this particularly. If they write about, say, love and forgiveness, then they meet with experiences which test, to its utmost, their power to love and forgive. If they write about faith, then circumstances will arise which test their faith, straining it almost to breaking point.

I must warn you, at this point, not to attempt to go ahead too quickly. Some in their desire to find God are so anxious to push on they pray for any suffering or experience if only, out of the fiery trial, they may be brought nearer and the more rapidly to God. This is almost certain to bring down on their heads such a series of difficult happenings as well-nigh to overwhelm them and strain them almost to breaking point. The Regenerative Life is quite strenuous enough without this. If we are willing to be led entirely by the Spirit and that God's will should be done; and if our prayer is "Lead Thou me on", then we get all the experiences that we need, and they come to us just at the right moment.

The simple way of attainment is to live *the Life*: that is, the life of faith and love, following our Lord Jesus Christ in all things. Whatever experiences are attracted to us must be *worked through*, and not avoided, or "wiped out" by mental treatments, in the way practised by metaphysicians. There is always some lesson to be learnt in our experiences, and if we work through them, we are greatly benefited by so doing; in fact, this is the only way by which we can become perfected.

God has appointed one way whereby we can cease to be sons of mortality, being changed into Immortal Children of Heaven; and this is regeneration as taught and lived by our Lord Jesus Christ. The soul has to be impregnated by the Immortal Life of God. We have to become filled with the Holy Ghost. We have to become changed entirely, being inwardly wrought upon by Heavenly and Divine Forces. We have to become sanctified, until at last, through the Grace of God, we become perfected. During this process of change the old nature has to be broken down, so as to allow the new nature to grow in its place. This may be accomplished in two ways:

> 1. By waiting repeatedly upon God, casting ourselves continually upon Him in utter abandonment.

> 2. Through experience.

These are the principal ways, but every act of our life has a bearing upon the new regenerative changes which take place within. The spiritual life is not something apart from our practical, everyday life, but the two are bound up together, and are really one. Doing an unpleasant task, in order to help someone more tired than ourselves, has a definite bearing on our ultimate attainment. Refusing to retaliate when others injure us, or are unkind to us, is also another important step forward in the new and wonderful journey towards eternal divine unity upon which we have entered.

It is the same with the two main methods, waiting upon God and passing through necessary experiences. They are bound up together and intermingled, so to speak. They act and re-act upon one another. Waiting upon God not only strengthens and changes us, but it also attracts to us experiences necessary for our development and regenerative transmutation. These experiences, in turn, cause us to wait upon God still more, and to cast ourselves upon Him with less reserve and greater abandon. This, in turn, attracts other experiences, all of which help to break down the old man and build up the new. Thus, a circle is established that is wholly beneficial to us, spiritually, this beneficent circle greatly accelerates our regeneration, hastening the time when the journey is run and the battle ended, not through death, but through victorious attainment, sanctification, and the overcoming of the self or "natural" man. All this is accomplished, not of ourselves, but through the Holy Spirit, the new Comforter whom Our Lord sent to finish and carry on His redeeming work in our heart and life.

This beneficent "circle" has its negative counterpart. If we sin, or if we become slack in spiritual matters, or fall asleep spiritually, then some trouble or disaster is needed in order to wake us up again and get us going in the straight and narrow path. Therefore, the more we "slack", the greater the number of troubles of this kind that we attract to ourselves. Thus, the only thing for us to do is to go forward, keeping pace with our unfoldment or inward growth.

When our Lord was perfected, he became "Called of God an high priest after the order of Melchizedek". (See Hebrews, V. 8, 9, 10). In the same way we have to be perfected and sanctified, after which we too are made kings and priests unto God. See Rev. 1., 6. Not High Priests, but priests. Our Lord is our High Priest, the Priest of priests, as well as Lord of Lords, and King of Kings.

Now the office of a priest, in this interior sense, is a very sacred one. A real priest is a mediator between God and man. He takes the spiritual gifts and truths of Heaven and passes them on to those committed to his charge. He is a miniature Christ, for we are all destined to attain, if we faint not, unto the measure of the stature of the fullness of Christ. (Ephesians IV., 13.)

About the 7th and last stage nothing can be said by one who has not yet attained thereto. But, if I had attained, I should say nothing, because it is too sacred, and even if I tried to do so, I could not say a word, for no one can describe the indescribable. Swedenborg likens the seven stages of regeneration to the seven days of creation, and no doubt there must be a close correspondence. It was on the 7th day that God rested from His labours. It is at the 7th stage that man rests from his, for the conflict is over and the Sabbath of the soul's experience is his to enjoy.

It is in this way, the way of regeneration, that the Lord, by His Holy Spirit, brings us out of bondage into His glorious liberty: raises us from sin and mortality into His Light and Eternal Life: changes us from natural men, children of darkness and death, into celestial beings, sons and daughters of the Most High.

> To him that overcometh will I give to eat of the hidden manna, and will give him a white stone, and in the stone a new name written, which no man knoweth saving he that receiveth it.
>
> Rev. 2, 17.

A Guide to Right Thinking in Action

Practical Applications and Examples of Right Thinking

Hamblin Vision Publishing

Chapter Thirteen

But what IS Right Thinking?

Right thinking in a broad, elementary and general sense, is thinking positive thoughts instead of negative ones. It means entertaining thoughts of success instead of failure, health instead of sickness, love instead of hate, cheerfulness instead of gloom, optimism instead of pessimism, opulence instead of poverty, victory instead of defeat, liberty instead of bondage, and so on. One who does this becomes inwardly changed. Through being changed inwardly, one's actions also become altered, this, in turn, transforms our life and circumstances. Therefore, through the change from wrong to right thinking, the character or self becomes altered, hence the scripture fulfils itself: "Be ye transformed by the renewing of your mind".

Right thinking, however, in its highest sense, is something even greater than all this. It is thinking in an altogether higher consciousness and from an entirely new [to the individual] standpoint. It means thinking from the perspective of the universal Mind instead of the weak, limited, finite mind. It means thinking in the *actual consciousness* of love as the *reality*, perfection as the *reality*, health as the *reality*, harmony as the *reality*. It means liberation in thought from being enslaved by the senses and the desires. It means living the life in a higher octave, upon an altogether higher plane. In other words, it is possible to rise above the limitations of time and sense; to aspire to the consciousness of eternal life and being; to think *with* God instead of in the human finite way which is against Him.

Right thinking is also thinking and living in the consciousness that all is well. It is to know in *one's very soul*, that God's ways are perfect; that He makes no mistakes; that everything is working together towards the complete fulfilment of the divine Purpose. Right thinking also is to know that perfection exists as a reality *now*, and to think in the consciousness of this knowledge.

It must not be thought, however, that entering this higher consciousness turns us into some supreme being, because this is very far from being the case, but it does give us that revelation of truth which Jesus said should make us free. The difference between thinking with the finite limited mind and thinking with the universal mind is perfectly described in Isaiah, chapter 55: "For my thoughts are not your thoughts. Neither are your ways my ways, saith the Lord. For as the Heavens are higher than the earth, so are my ways higher than your ways, and my thoughts than your thoughts". Therefore, in order to think *with* God, which is the aim of every seeker after truth, it is necessary to rise high above the ordinary plane of human thought and to think in an altogether higher consciousness. Man, when he is ready for the change, is invited by God to make this change. In the same chapter we read: "Let the wrongdoer forsake his way, and the unrighteous man forsake his thoughts and let him return unto the Lord, and He will have mercy upon him; and to our God for He will abundantly pardon".

That it is possible to reach this cosmic or universal mind is abundantly proved both by human experience and in the New Testament. That Jesus the Christ could rise, at will, into this super-conscious realm of the universal mind is perfectly evident. His teaching, for the most part, is given direct from the cosmic mind and standpoint, and is only understandable when this fact is recognised and understood. Undoubtedly, he taught his disciples that it was possible also for them to rise into this higher mind of God.

It is from this higher plane or octave that all healing is done; it is from this superconscious realm that truth can be understood in such a way as to set us free.

Right thinking is the very reverse of impractical dreaming or mystical ecstasy. It is intensely practical. I can say, as a practical businessman[1] who started life without a penny, and who had a rough and tumble fight with the difficulties and realities of life for many years, that there is nothing so practically helpful as right thinking. Having had to make my own way in life from a very early age

---

1. Detailed more fully in *"The Story of my Life"* by Henry Thomas Hamblin.

without the help of either monetary influence or education, in addition to being handicapped by delicate health, nothing appeals to me that will not "cut ice". Before I can accept anything, I must prove its practical, definite usefulness.

The good effects which follow this higher right thinking in harmony with God, are described in poetic and symbolic language by the inspired prophet, Isaiah, who himself is speaking from the standpoint of the universal Mind. Isaiah says: "For ye shall go out with joy and be led forth with peace; the mountains and the hills shall break forth before you into singing, and all the trees of the field shall clap their hands. Instead of the thorn shall come up the fir tree, and instead of the brier shall come up the myrtle tree; and it shall be to the Lord for a name, for an everlasting sign that shall not be cut off".

All the above promises have been proved, in practical experience, to be perfectly true. Those who learn this art and science of right thinking find, in course of time, that the thorns and briers or failure, fear, discord, hate, sickness, unhappiness and needless suffering, give place to true success, achievement, harmony, love, happiness and health. The prophet's words, when reduced to plain, ordinary language, clearly indicate that for those who think and act in harmony with God, instead of against Him, shall, here and now, in this life, enjoy harmony, peace, health, happiness and joy.

And it is far more than this, as the following pages will show. It brings with it a new conception of life. It says in effect that life is spiritual, that you cannot separate matter and spirit. It was

Thomas Carlyle who said that matter could only exist spiritually, therefore man must exist spiritually or not at all. In fact, man is a spirit, and the physical body is merely his material and outward expression. If life is spiritual, then man can be truly successful through spiritual forces; he can be healthy through spiritual forces; he can achieve and accomplish through spiritual forces; he can be happy through spiritual forces; he can love through spiritual forces. Therefore, the true art of living is the development, training and use of spiritual powers. There is no method of education that does this; it can never be achieved by objective means; it can be accomplished only by subjective processes. By "spiritualized" right thinking it is possible to arouse and train man's inward powers so that he can achieve success in life, bring harmony into his home, health to his body, and by his joy and optimism bring brightness and happiness to all his companions. And more - it will enable him to unfold, to find within him the spark of divinity which for so long has been hidden.

This science and art of right thinking is also practical. It has taken a great truth and, brushing aside all that is not essential, has woven it into a practical system which can be applied with precision to all the problems of life. It has discovered that life is a result, an effect, and that the reality and cause are within. It teaches that life responds to certain laws, and that by working in harmony with these laws results can be obtained with mathematical precision. It disperses the vagueness, mystery and uncertainty which surround so many teachings, and shows how life can be governed by scientific methods. It teaches that the running of the universe is not whimsical but governed by immutable laws. "As a man soweth that shall he also reap" and "As a man thinketh in his heart so is he", are proved to be scientifically true. Just as man can harness the lightning, drive his trains and machinery by electricity, and light his streets and houses, so can man, when he understands the laws which govern his life, produce results nonetheless remarkable, and which can be predicted with equal certainty, because they are the effects of certain causes. We no longer need to feel fated or victimised by circumstances as we try to walk the mysterious path of life in darkness and uncertainty, relying upon chance or upon knowledge and understanding. Instead, we can govern our life with precision and certainty, and in this knowledge, there is inner peace.

The importance of right thinking lies in the fact that all that we are ourselves, together with what comes into our life, are largely the result of our thoughts. It has been said that "we are what we think we are". It was Buddha who said: "All that we are is the result of what we have thought; it is founded on our thoughts; it is made-up of our thoughts". The ancient Upanishad says: "What a man thinks, that he becomes". James Allen wrote: "Your own thoughts, desires and inspirations comprise your world, and, to you, all that there is in the universe of beauty and joy and bliss, or of ugliness and sorrow and pain, is contained within yourself. By your own thoughts you make or mar your life, your world, your universe".

If our life is unhappy and "out of sync" today, it is largely due to our wrong and disharmonious thinking in the past, the fruits of which we have to bear now. Every disharmonious thought brings, with mathematical exactness, its corresponding result. We cannot escape the effects of our thoughts for they come to us with perfect precision. "Whatsoever a man soweth that shall he also reap" is written in letters of gold on the portals of eternity, and it is so because the universe is not run by chance, but by exact and never failing nor varying law. Therefore, if our life is disharmonious, it is simply the effect of our thoughts, for everyone gets exactly the experience he needs. He who indulges in self-pity is wasting his energy for whatever comes into his life is the exact result of his thoughts.

But you exclaim: "What about actions? What about sin? My reply is that actions and sin are simply the result of wrong thinking. If we think evil, we express evil. If we allow wrong thoughts to enter our mind, they birth bitter fruits in due season. Wrong thinking is thinking out of harmony with eternal truth and is responsible for much ill health, restriction and unhappiness, as well as wrong actions of many kinds.

Some may say: "Well if we cannot escape the effect of our thought, we may as well give up trying, and then where does your philosophy of joy come in?" The answer is that one's thoughts, as the result of self-training and self-discipline, can be controlled. Some people may say that it cannot be done; that thought is so elusive it cannot be controlled. Others will say: "I cannot control my thoughts; If

I could, I would cease to worry. As it is, as soon as the slightest trouble appears, I start worrying and fearing, and although I know that I'm not doing any good by this, but rather harm, I cannot help myself", or "I am of a worrying nature". But that does not prove that thought cannot be controlled. It only proves that the speakers have not understood the art of scientific thought control. Thought can be controlled as result of perseverance, patience and persistence. Great changes such as this cannot be accomplished in a day, but they can be achieved in course of time by systematic practice of right principles.

Granted then that it is possible to control your thoughts, let us consider the results which will accrue if right thinking is practised

First, instead of destructive thinking there will be constructive thinking. Instead of struggling against life and creating difficult future conditions, the life and character will be built up in beauty and harmony. Instead of creating disharmony, a hostile environment, failure, and disease there will be a tendency to change these things into success, health, happiness, peace and joy.

Second, the powerful vibrations of constructive thinking i.e. , thinking in harmony with the infinite and universal Mind, will gradually change the character and transform the life. Harmony will be restored through thinking in line with eternal truth. The infinitely good life force, which is the life of God, immanent in man will be allowed to manifest itself in consciousness in the form of good, such as health, harmony, achievement through service, efficiency, and sufficiency.

Life is not robbed of its discipline, but of its disharmonies and unnecessary suffering. Right thinking, that is, thinking from the perspective of truth, restores harmony, which is the normal condition. Good is positive, not a negative condition. Unfortunately, most people's idea of "good" is entirely negative. To them "good" is merely an absence of anything unpleasant. For instance, their idea of health is absence of disease; and happiness, to them, is mere absence of unhappiness. They know nothing of the abounding joy of health or the bubbling joy of the new life. God's life is perfect and, if allowed to flow unimpeded, can only manifest in the form of good. It is wrong thinking, false beliefs and absence of truth, that divert the good stream of God's perfect life into disharmonious channels, producing disease, poverty and other negative conditions.

Many people needlessly fear the effects of past wrong thinking and wrong actions. They say: "This is my karma; I must live it out". They become so saturated with this idea they aggravate and increase their troubles. Yet, if they would but believe the truth and realise and think and live in the consciousness of truth, they would find their troubles greatly lessened, if not altogether removed. It is useless to fight against life, but by meeting each difficulty with truth, and by thinking from the standpoint of truth, and living in the consciousness of truth, the life becomes transformed, and all its difficulties turn out to be friends in disguise. Additionally, as the character becomes changed, exterior influences and vibrations affect one less and less. Their power to hurt decreases as we rise to higher vibrations.

CHAPTER FOURTEEN

The Effect Of Thought

The immediate effect of thought upon our body, spirit, work, happiness, in fact every department of life, is so obvious that it seems hardly necessary to touch upon it. But experience with my students in the past has convinced me that some people are not awake to the power that thought exerts over their actions, and consequently over all that is the result of their actions. Therefore, it may not be out of place if I touch lightly upon this subject.

A thought, someone has said, is an action in the process of being born. Everything that we do is the result of thoughts entertained or held in the mind. We may do things on the impulse of the moment, but that impulse is the result of a thought or thoughts previously held in the mind.

The subconscious mind is a centre of extraordinary energy and power. It is a blind force and acts upon suggestion. In other words, it acts upon the impressions which it receives from the objective mind, and it depends upon whether these impressions, thoughts or suggestions are good or bad as to what sort of action the subconscious mind is going to bring forth in the life. The will and the moral sense must commence their defensive work with the thoughts and not with actions, because the former are the cause of the latter.

If therefore, one holds thoughts of a selfish character in the mind, then selfish actions will manifest in the life; if thoughts of pessimism, then failure will be expressed; if thoughts of sickness and disease, then they will manifest in real sickness and disease in the body. If say a young person says: "I don't think I can do a certain task", he will fail, but if instead he assures himself that he can do it, then his subconscious mind will do all it possibly can to help him succeed, and unless he attempts something far beyond his stage of development, he will accomplish it. Good thoughts will produce good actions, and bad thoughts bad actions, and it is by controlling the thoughts that self-mastery is to be found. All bad habits in the life and body have their origin in bad habits of thought, and good habits can be built up only by constructive, positive thinking, accompanied by corresponding right action.

If you say on a wet morning: "Isn't it a horrible morning!", then you make it a horrible morning for yourself and also help to make it unpleasant for other people, because you are not only sending an oppressive suggestion to your own subconscious mind, but you are doing the same to those who hear you. On the other hand, if you will take up the attitude that the weather might be a lot worse, that the rain is needed in the country, that the sun is shining gloriously behind the clouds and that everything is perfect in God's perfect world, you will transform the day into one of pleasure.

Your own inner radiance and sense of joy cannot help but uplift those around you.

In the same way if you say to yourself: "I feel very bad today", then the subconscious mind acts accordingly. The message goes out to the millions of industrious little workers whose duty is the repairing, building up and keeping the body healthy, and they act accordingly. The whole system becomes depressed, the vitality is lowered, the powers of resistance weakened, so that you become easy prey to the first infection that you encounter. On the other hand, if when you feel off colour, you breathe deeply and as you breathe in affirm: "The Infinite is my health" and hold in the mind a thought or picture of perfect health, you will find that your condition will improve. The message of perfect health will be sent telepathically all over the body, and all the tiny fighters and workers will be inspired and encouraged to work on your behalf.

Again, in the same way, one who says: "I am sure competition will ruin my business", is suggesting to himself his own failure. All his actions will unconsciously be directed to this end, and time will inevitably see the extinction of his business. Yet a person in similar circumstances who states: "No competition will be able to affect my business. I will make my goods or my services so good that all my customers will, for their own sakes, continue to deal with me", because he is inspired by his own suggestion, he will work to make his services so indispensable to the public that his business will succeed more than ever.

By this, we can see how thoughts affect our lives, and how it is only by controlling the thoughts that the actions can be governed, and through the actions the very life and environment itself.

Right thinking goes far more deeply into this great subject than this. It teaches that thoughts held in the mind attract, by the law of vibration, the material for their objective expression. That actually what is held in the mind, with fine clarity of thought and inward vision, becomes manifested in the life; that each type of thought brings forth fruit of its very nature. It teaches that if there is confusion of thought in the mind, there is experienced confusion and disharmony in the life and circumstances, and that according to the thought and mental vision the life is either broken or blessed.

The practice of right thinking, additionally trains the mind to think only those thoughts which will harmonise with the immutable laws which govern the universe, bringing into the life the highest good, truest joy, the only satisfying success[1].

---

1. For an explanation of greater depth, read *The Power of Thought* by H.T. Hamblin, available from www.thehamblinvision.org.uk

Chapter Fifteen

The Greatest Achievement

The greatest message that this book brings to you is this: that we can, by working daily for a short time in the inner and higher mental and spiritual realm, subtract evil from our lives and add good in its place. That is to say, by meditating upon the divine Perfection we become changed into its likeness. This will also destroy that influence in life which we call bad luck and ill fortune and replace it by certain and harmonious good. It will banish unhappiness and fill us with a great joy which has its source within and is not dependent upon outside circumstances. We can protect ourselves and others from danger, difficulty and disaster. We work with precision; we are not dealing with uncertain theories, but with immutable law which can never fail or alter. This is real prayer.

We do not do this by willpower; we do it by harmonising with the Infinite. Real success in life is only to be found along this line of harmony with the Divine. Humans are spiritual beings, and when we realise our own spiritual nature and learn how to draw upon the infinite powers within us by working in unity with Divine Source, our lives becomes changed. Day by day a little negativity is taken out of our lives, and day by day a little good is put in its place. Results are not seen at first, but they are cumulative, and in time are bound to manifest just as surely as the rising and setting of the sun.

Many people say: "What is this negative influence that follows me? As soon as I get on a little in business, I suffer a severe loss. When I make plans for a happy life, disaster overtakes me and shatters all my hopes". There is nothing bad or negative following us; instead, what we are suffering from is absence of good due to the disharmony of our thoughts and lives. When once the disharmony gives place to unity, then the transformation of the life begins.

But while any true system of thought control is training the student in these major things, it is also accomplishing minor changes, which make for success and stability in life. Willpower, concentration, determination, perseverance, creative imagination, directed thinking, natural memory, the appreciation of beauty, self-confidence, cheerfulness and optimism, are all developed without the student being aware of it. I mention these things because they are of real value to the student, but they fade into insignificance beside the major objects which the practice of truth achieves.

Right thinking brings accuracy and precision into the life. It makes life certain and secure. It brings everything down to a system, a system which, if followed, gives mathematically certain results. By that I do not mean that it is wise to always decide for yourself what form "good" shall take in your life; for it is very often better to leave this to the divine Mind. But the certainty and exactitude is in this, that by working steadily, persistently, and daily through the avenue of controlled, directed thought, towards the source of all, from which everything proceeds, one is able to transmute negative life experience into positive energy. At first the old troubles and evils persist, with some they even get a little worse, but after a time it is noticed that the attacks are less severe, the trouble less acute, and from then onwards a steady and gradual improvement takes place, until the whole life and circumstances are transformed.

Chapter Sixteen

Happiness

Happiness is an inward mental state. It cannot be found in outward things. The idea popular with the masses that happiness is to be found in material possessions, in wealth, the means of gratification and luxury, is not shared by those who possess these things. The supposed happiness which the unthinking imagine is to be obtained by wealth and all that wealth can buy, is merely the glittering baubles of life towards which men stretch out eager hands, but which ever eludes their grasp.

Henry Victor Morgan in an exalted moment once wrote:

> Today on the heights I stand
> Above the sea of thought,
> And look o'er the changing drift
> At the baubles for which men fought;
> That slip through their clinging hands
> And ever remain uncaught.
> Unchained through the drift of years.
> They float o'er the surface clear;

> And for ever warm hands reach out
> As the illusions of life draw near;
> ill the weary hands sink deep
> And the eager new appear.

Happiness, then, is not to be secured by chasing the illusions of life, but by looking within where the only true reality lies.

We are spiritual beings here and now, and our unhappiness is due to our lack of appreciation of this great fact. We will always be unsatisfied until we realise that we are spiritual beings, gifted with godlike powers; that we, as spirit, are one with the infinite Spirit, the Source of all things.

When we realise this astounding fact, the heavy load of care which has oppressed us, the sense of our own loneliness and friendlessness, the uncertainty and futility of life, all disperse, and we realise for the first time the true inward meaning of happiness.

Happiness does not depend upon circumstances. The unenlightened say: "If only my circumstances were better, I should be happy", yet if their circumstances were altered, they would still be unhappy. Circumstances are not the cause of unhappiness but are the effect of the same cause; they are the result of a lack of adjustment, and of an inward spiritual disharmony. The change within which will cure our unhappiness will cause the unhappy circumstances to disperse also, for as soon as the lesson is learned and the necessary inward adjustment made, their mission is finished. To long for painful experiences to pass away in order that one may be happy is futile; the only way is to seek for the cause of the trouble within and make the necessary adjustment to life and the universe. One who is unhappy is out of harmony with the eternal Will and the divine scheme, and the unpleasant circumstances not only are the result of a wrong attitude of the soul, but they also seek to make one realise the cause, and to adjust the life accordingly. Happiness comes from within; it is the effect of harmonious adjustment with life; of coming into line with the divine will and purpose. Do not think for a moment that the divine purpose is that our life should be boring, unhappy, painful or lacking in abundance and good. It may appear uninviting, but this is merely an illusion, for it leads to joy unspeakable, and happiness which cannot be described.

Again, there can be no happiness without service. To live a self-centred, selfish life is the way of disintegration and death. It is the certain road to unhappiness, dissatisfaction and despair. Service to the whole, to life, to God, to humanity, to the universe, this is the way of harmony and inner satisfaction. No-one who is self-centred can be happy, for such a one is out of harmony with the divine Idea. Neither can he be at peace who carries out his daily work grudgingly. But one who works for the whole and makes his daily work a sweet offering of love to all life and humanity, enters the divine harmony; he knows what true happiness is.

Also, in order to be happy, one must be able to exercise thought control. It is obvious that if happiness is an inward mental state, thought must have a lot to do with it. Those who cannot control their thoughts give way to fear and worry, or hate and anger, depression and gloom, and when this is the case happiness is impossible. One who does not make use of thought control is affected adversely by circumstances, by the disappointments and trials and testing times of life. But one who can control her thoughts is unaffected by these things. She can steer her thoughts away from dwelling upon everything negative and instead keep them fixed upon the one great positive reality of the universe - the infinite spirit of good and perfection. By doing this she loses all fear and unhappiness; she enters into infinite peace and joy. She leaves her weaknesses behind her, and filled with divine power, lives a life of tranquillity and victory.

Chapter Seventeen

Power

To the uninitiated, life is so material it is difficult to believe that behind the visible universe is a transcendental world of spirit which is the perfect reality of which the objective world is but an expression. Yet, this is true. The visible world, beautiful as it is, and marred though it may be by man's disharmony, is merely an effect or expression of the infinite reality. Metaphysicians who say that matter and the material universe do not exist, do so because, in a philosophical sense, only that which is permanent and unchanging can be said to exist. As far as this consciousness goes, however, the visible exists. If I have an abscess as large as my fist at the back of my neck, then, as far as this consciousness is concerned that abscess exists. It exists in my consciousness for a time and cannot be entirely ignored. On the one hand we have abstract thinkers who say that nothing material has any existence. Yet we also have concrete thinkers, materialists if you like, who cannot believe in anything that is not tangible. The truth is somewhere between the two. These are two halves to the complete whole. There is the unseen permanent reality, and there is the changing expression of that reality. There is the divine Idea, and there is the unfoldment of that perfection through endless change and evolution in material form. Matter is a vehicle of God's expression. It clothes His idea in form and colour. It is the outer garment of the spirit. To ignore either the material or the spiritual is to delude ourselves; they *together* form the One complete whole. In either case we ignore God, for God is the Creator of His universe; it is formed out of His spiritual substance; God's thought finds expression in His creation, therefore, to deny matter and to call it evil is to deny God and call Him evil. Here, it might be appropriate to add that God is transcendent as well as immanent. In one sense, God is expressed in His universe, yet in another sense, He is not, for He is ever beyond it.

Matter then, and the material universe, are ever changing effects, ever evolving, ever unfolding more perfectly the divine Idea. The tremendous power that works through the universe is spiritual; it is the divine Mind in motion. This power is infinite; its object is to express on this material plane a perfect manifestation of the divine Idea. Its object is not to manifest disease, ill health, unhappiness, poverty, wrongdoing, rather it is ever seeking to express itself in perfect health and harmony. The fact that there is unhappiness, sickness and poverty in the world only proves that man is out of harmony with his divine Source. Instead of divine life forces being allowed to flow freely and manifest good, they are diverted and made to produce negativity. The secret of all healing and true achievement is to remove the barriers which divert the spiritual forces of life, thus opening the life to the divine inflow.

This power is infinite; It flows in a constant stream from the unseen spiritual source into the material universe. We see it manifested in myriad forms, for God is immanent everywhere in His universe. We can look into the patient eyes of our animal friends and see Him there; we can gaze in rapture at the loveliness of a simple flower, or the grandeur of a crimson sunset and behold the beauty of His character. God is everywhere and in everything; to know this is to enter a new life of fullness and joy. We see the infinite Power manifested in all the wonders of the universe; in the evolution of worlds and system of worlds; in the immense power of nature; in the life which repeats itself through the ages.

In man, God enters into a new relationship with His creation. In man are the possibilities of a wider and deeper consciousness. Man stands at the apex of creation; he is the highest product of nature. All the kingdoms combine to produce him: mineral, vegetable and animal all minister to him and own him as Lord of creation. Man's feet are on the earth and his head in the heavens; he has within him, still lying latent, the possibilities of Godhood. He alone of all creation can think with God, commune with Him, enter into His consciousness, and become, in the course of time, one with the Infinite.

Humankind, being what it is, can draw upon this infinite power in a special way. We can, through the divine power of his mind and thought, consciously identify ourselves with the Infinite and draw unlimited power from his divine Source. There is no height to which we cannot climb if we will only keep our faces to the "light" and draw upon the inexhaustible fountains of God. "All power is given unto me in heaven and in earth", said Jesus, and of us, his weaker brothers, the same glorious fact is true. Man has thought himself to be a worm, but this is true only of his finite false personality; actually, he is called to be a king and priest unto God. Man thinks he is a creature of a moment; he gropes about in the ashes of his material life while above him is the glorious crown of his divine heritage. He languishes in weakness when he might instead be filled with infinite power.

The power is infinite, it is in you and in me; it is in all people. Very few know of this power, a still smaller number know how to *use* it. The majority would be very surprised, if not shocked, were you to tell them that within them lie dormant infinite and divine powers, that within each of them is a spark of the divine fire, an inherent perfection which is patiently seeking expression. Yet, this is true; the power within us is infinite. It is divine. It can revolutionise you if you will but realise its presence and allow it freedom of expression.

The power is the same as it was in the days of miracles; the law does not change. Those who adjust their lives in such a way as to bring them into harmony with the divine Law are healed. They express more and more of the infinite perfection, not just in their body, but also in their character. The power is the same, no matter how it is employed. It can be used to strengthen the body, give power to the mind, or bring the highest achievement into the life. No one who draws upon the infinite power and wisdom can ever be a failure; his life reflects the infinite achievement of God.

Chapter Eighteen

True Prosperity

The true prosperity is not the accumulation of great wealth. To be truly prosperous is to have the use of enough to enable one to live without struggling and yet to be free from the joyless burden of wealth. The truly wise is one who chooses to have enough and yet not too much, for while too little is irksome, to possess wealth is to assume burdens and responsibilities which are not worthwhile.

Some readers will raise the moral question of whether it is right to be even comfortably well off while so many are in need. This is, of course, a question for each individual to settle for himself. Personally, I think one is justified in accepting from life enough material things to enable one to develop and unfold on all planes, physical, mental and spiritual. One is therefore entitled to receive all that is necessary for one's highest development if one is prepared to give one's best services in exchange to humankind and the world. One who gives her best service, her best thoughts, her best emotions to life, the world and her fellows, is entitled to an adequate return in the form of the best that life can give. But he who thinks he is "clever" and by cunning tries to cheat life and his fellow man, taking much and giving little or nothing in return is not really clever, but only foolish, for what he gains in one direction he loses in another. He may gain money, true, but loses all the best and most satisfying qualities and gifts of life. Ones which money cannot buy. The way to true prosperity is through highest service, a changed dominant note of the inner mind, and understanding of truth through right thinking. This brings us into line with the divine law of giving and receiving; it also removes the mental cause of lack and poverty. This brings into the life a wise opulence, neither too much nor too little, and the sure knowledge that we can never lack any good thing.

One who does not understand the working of the divine Law is always afraid of poverty. He may be passing rich, yet, at the back of his mind is the haunting fear that he may lose it all and come into need. He so fears the future and what it may bring that he must hoard up money; something to fall back upon if things go wrong. Not satisfied with what he already has, he strives after greater riches in order to make himself "safe". This is the worship of mammon. So long as we look to money and material means in themselves as our source of supply, so long as we think that these things keep us from want, we serve mammon and therefore cannot serve God.

One who acknowledges that God (universal Mind and Spirit, if you prefer the term) is the Source of all supply, and daily and hourly realises his oneness with this infinite Source, can never lack any good thing. All that she need trouble about is to see that she gives her best and most efficient service to life in exchange for the abundance that she receives. One who cannot yet see God's bounty visible in his life should act, as far as service and thankfulness are concerned, as though it were already in manifestation. It is sure to come sooner or later, that is, if fear thoughts and limitation thoughts are transmuted into thoughts of God's plenty, as the reality, behind the lack and poverty of the unreality. This is the *true* prosperity - the *real* opulence.

It must not be thought, however, that one can sit still while the best things of life drop into one's lap. One must first be active mentally and spiritually in the inner world of thought and then work physically. Life is mainly action; therefore, to be worthy of prosperity one must work. Work, when well loved, is one of the greatest joys of life. No one can be happy or healthy who does not engage in plenty of work, not directed merely to his own selfish ends, but work given as an offering of love to life and the world.

It is not claimed that right thinking will suddenly convert a poor person into a rich one, neither does it dangle a get-rich-quick scheme before you. But it does train you to stop attracting poverty into your life, and instead put you on the road which, if pursued, will lead to a carefree sufficiency. It does show you how to stop the negative habit of thought and negative mental attitude which, by their vibration, keep success away. It also shows you how to enter into harmony with immutable law and, consequently, come under the law of attraction. It does show you how to do something with your mind which will take a little negativity and poverty out of your life and put a little good and prosperity back into it instead. This enacted several times a day will have a cumulative effect on the life which will in time begin to manifest itself and increase from year to year.

Some of my readers who are idealists may say that, if they accept more than a mere pittance for their work, they will have more than their fair share and consequently rob the poor. Yet, in reality, this is far from being the case. Our source of supply is spiritual and not material. God is not poverty stricken. He is infinite abundance itself. As children of God, all the abundance of God is ours, not for selfish use or enjoyment, but for the use of and service to the whole. The conditions of our lives are an outward expression of our thoughts and attitude of mind. If our thoughts forever centre round a belief in lack and limitation, then these things manifest in the outward life, for the outward life reflects our thought life. Our outward life is largely composed of our thoughts clothed in material form. It is not the reality. The reality is perfect. Your life and mine are imaged in God's mind as perfect. By wrong thinking and false beliefs, we hide the truth from ourselves, thus manifesting imperfection instead of perfection. Perfection, however, is still the only reality, and all imperfection is caused by a materialisation of our thoughts which hide the truth from us. Our life has always been imaged in the divine Mind as perfect, even before the beginning of time, and all our needs are abundantly supplied and always will be, even when time itself shall cease to be. The object of our teaching is to bring those who are willing to the stage known as realisation. At this stage the truth is understood by the soul, the

Kingdom is found, after which "all these things shall be added unto you".

A practical application of the teaching of Jesus is the only way by which the problem of supply can be solved for all time, once and for all. When once we find the Kingdom, we find that all our needs are supplied at just the right time, according to our faith and understanding.

If we look at nature around us, we find no evidence of poverty in the divine Idea. Everywhere we see prodigal abundance and lavish profusion. Thousands of acorns to form a single oak; and enough energy devoted to flowers alone to clothe every son of man in material plenty. God is not poverty stricken, and those who enter into harmony with the divine Idea can never lack any good thing.

Some of us may feel that we are beaten in the selfish battle for material existence. The egocentric and ruthless may elbow us aside, trample on us, and make off with that which we would like for ourselves and our loved ones. We may feel that we are like sheep amongst wolves. This is very true; for spiritually-minded people are different from the worldly and generally are on the losing end if they adopt the worldly methods. Even if they succeed, they find that what they have won can be held only by strain, effort and force. Every man's hand is against them, and they experience friction continually.

Now, the true, spiritual way of working is to seek the prosperity that comes from the Infinite, or what the Old Testament would call the blessing of the Lord. When God, or the Spirit is blessing us, or when we are in harmony with spiritual law, prosperity comes to us without effort and strain. It comes gently, like the falling of a soft rain. Unlike the prosperity of the materialists it does not bring unhappiness and disillusion, but rather harmony and peace. God wants us to live happy, free, healthy and joyous lives, and if we obey His laws, He adds his blessing in the form of a prosperity that brings no care or sorrow but only adds to our harmony and joy.

In order that there should be no misunderstanding, let me say that this is entirely different from the method of visualising what you want and compelling it to appear. This method, which involves the will, is a lower form of psychism and it is not a spiritual way of working. Although it may appear to be successful, it invokes the law of karma along with all that is involved.

Chapter Nineteen

Health and Healing

Health is the birthright of every human being. If we are sick, diseased, or suffering from prolonged ill health, it is because we are out of harmony with the divine plan. The vigorous health of our ancestors is gradually giving way to a more fragile health because man is becoming more sensitive mentally and spiritually. Therefore, he depends more and more upon mental and spiritual forces for his life and health. In actuality, we are becoming more nervous and highly strung, more imaginative, more sensitive to the power of thought and other spiritual and psychic forces. This is why man must look more and more to the one Source of life for his health, energy and vitality.

Right thinking carries a message of health. It maintains that this mysterious thing which we call "life" is a manifestation of God, and that it is only by going right back to the first cause, the Source of all life, and adjusting our lives into harmony with spiritual laws, and by identifying ourselves consciously with this infinite power, that we can find true healing. Once this is done, disease and ill health pass away, not to reappear in another form, but leave the life for ever.

But it must not be thought that health is simply the absence of disease, for it is far more than this. To be well implies a certain flexibility of spirits, or possession of tremendous energy or at least a supply sufficient for all your needs. It means being fit and alive and full of joy both in work and play. One is in tune with the whole universe as well as one with the Source of all Life and infinite good.

To one who has gained perfect health by spiritual means, all things are indeed divine. Every blade of grass, every opening flower, the nodding trees, the whispering breeze, all speak to her soul and fill her heart with ecstasy and infinite content. Not only can we, through coming into harmony with the divine Source, become healthy, we can also help others to attain better health. I do not say that everyone possesses all the qualities necessary to become a successful spiritual healer, but everyone who finds health himself can also teach others to do the same.

CHAPTER TWENTY

Absolute Certainty

There is no chance or luck in the universe, all is unfailing law. The old idea of appeasing an angry deity is founded upon ignorance of this divine law. Fortunately for us, there is no condition or favour; all is according to immutable law and absolute justice. Divine spitefulness and divine favouritism do not exist, but eternal justice reigns supreme. We cannot curry divine favour; we must stand on our own feet, and as we sow, so shall we also reap.

Fortunately for us, the universe is governed by Universal Law and Infinite Justice. This Law and principle never alter, never fail, and never cease to operate. We therefore have only to work in harmony with the divine Law to obtain absolute certain results. So long as we are ignorant of the Law and work against it, so will our lives be filled with discord and what is called bad luck. There will be no certainty about it, for sometimes things will run smoothly, and we will say "our luck is in"; then all at once troubles and disasters may come thick and fast, and we will say "our luck is out". But when we learn to know the Law and how to work in harmony with it, we begin to gain exact results. We may not be able to tell what exact form it will take, but we will know with absolute certainty that good will manifest in our life as a result of something which we have initiated in our thought world, and as a result of right decisions and right conduct. We may not know when it will be manifested, but we will know with certainty that it will be manifested. For example, someone may have suffered from a physical weakness or condition for 20 years or so, and in spite of innumerable consultations with specialists and every kind of treatment both orthodox and complementary have gained no relief, yet as soon as he brings his mind and life into harmony with the Divine and works daily in accordance with certain laws, then he can rest assured his condition will slowly improve. Although the improvement may be infinitesimal it is cumulative and therefore ongoing.

It is the same with our circumstances and environment; we can bring ourselves into harmony with the Infinite and through working daily in the inner world improve our circumstances in the outer world. So long as we obey the Law and work constructively on the inner level, results will keep accumulating until at last they manifest in the outward life. The results must come; Divine Law always responds. The power never ceases to operate; *God can never fail*.

I do not care how negative a person is, nor how unsuccessful he may have been, nor how weakened by sickness and bad habits he is; if such a one will persevere and work according to this divine

Law, and persist and keep on in spite of lack of visible results at first, he will surely succeed; *he can never fail*.

I know now, although I have not always known it, that if I pray in the right way, I can never really fail. Results *always* come with mathematical exactness; there is no human element in this Law; it is absolute; it is perfect; it is exact.

If I pray in the right way and act accordingly, only good can come to me. It may not always be according to my human idea; but will always be the very best for me, according to Infinite Wisdom.

CHAPTER TWENTY-ONE

Mastery Of Fate

> Again on the heights I stand,
> Where God's winds sing a lullaby,
> And no more I reach for the gleam
> Of the baubles for which men die -
> For I reach to the heart of God
> And Master of Fate am I.
>
> Henry Victor Morgan

What do we mean by fate? The simplest definition is that it is those events over which we have no control. The more we understand the power and effect of our thinking the less we find in our life that is out of our control. But still there are some things which appear to be quite unavoidable, for instance, our parents, date and place of birth, country of origin, death of relatives, and other big things in life. Then again, what man or woman is there who, having reached mid-life, has not passed through an experience which defied all his or her powers of mind, body and soul, all his or her wealth or means, the help of friends and even frenzied prayers? Most of us are compelled to acknowledge that life is too big for us to handle and that there are events in it that are beyond our power to control.

There are those, however, who go much further than this. There are learned people who say that nothing happens; that we merely come up against things. They say that life is like a journey on a train, say from London to Edinburgh. The argument is that when we start on the journey, Edinburgh and all that lies between, are in existence, and that the reason we cannot see them until we reach them is simply due to limitations of sight. In the same way, it is argued that all the events of our life are already in existence, but we only experience them as we are swept along by life to come up against them, one by one. The fact that we cannot see the end from the beginning is due to limitations of consciousness.

Then there are those who are learned and skilled in esoteric and occult science. And although I am not skilled in these things, neither do I wish to be, I have been interested enough to try to find out how far the claims of these people could be substantiated. Although very sceptical, I was forced to admit that up to a certain point, their calculations and inferences were correct. I have come to the conclusion that skilled astrologers can predict in a broad way what a person's life will be. In some cases, their calculations may even prove to be very accurate. But this applies only so long as a person allows himself to be a creature of impulse, and a victim of circumstances. Directly we look to God for help and raise our thoughts heavenwards, we rise above the influences and impulses which otherwise would make us fall into serious error and trouble. When we resist the temptation, in the strength of the Spirit through raising our thoughts to God, we break the bonds which bind us; that is, we become free from that predetermined life which the horoscope forecasts. Every time that we control our thoughts, refusing to let them run in one direction and compelling them to flow into a higher, more positive one, we break free from our bondage. In other words, *we master our fate*.

The life of the awakened man cannot be predicted. He becomes a liberated soul. He becomes freed from the law of sin and death. He strikes out on a new path of victory and overcoming.

Chapter Twenty-Two

Self Confidence

Lack of self-confidence is a cause of failure to many. They have the ability, they are ambitious, they have ideas, but they lack sufficient trust and belief in their own powers and ability to succeed, which is the priceless possession of all people of achievement.

All successful people are splendidly self-confident, and no one who does not possess this spiritual quality - for it is a spiritual quality - can ever succeed. I have never met a successful person yet who did not utterly and absolutely believe in himself or herself. Neither have I ever met an unsuccessful person who was not lacking in this quality.

Right thinking develops self-confidence in that it frees us from fear. What would some of us not give to free ourselves from fear and mistrust? Yet it can be done, and the process is not difficult. But far more important than this is the seeker learns to explore the wonders of his own interior mental and spiritual powers and gradually trains them and uses them. When the seeker discovers he or she can draw upon limitless powers, and can call upon inexhaustible resources, there develops within the mind confidence, certainty and a perfect trust in these inward powers. The seeker instead of saying, "Can I do it?" says, "I can do it", and believing what he says goes and does it, relying upon the inward power to carry him through, and this power *never fails.*

The inherently successful man believes in himself and because of that succeeds. The trained student believes in the unlimited powers of the universal Mind which he can, by using his powers of thought, call upon and use whenever he needs. In addition, he knows and understands the Law, and is prevented from making mistakes in life which those with less knowledge are liable to fall into and, consequently, make a mess of their lives. Therefore, knowledge of truth not only frees us from fear, making us more confident, it also imparts knowledge and wisdom by which the life can be guided into a lasting and abundant success.

When man realises his oneness with the Infinite, he can never fear lack of self-confidence. He knows that all the divine forces are his; they seek to obey his will and minister to him. Though his feet are still on the earth, his mind is in God; his heart thrills with a sense of universal and unlimited power.

Chapter Twenty-Three

Peace

The right-thinking philosophy is practical, and one of its most helpful teachings is that there is a higher mental realm into which, after a little practice one can attain. Furthermore, it is accessible to all who will persevere. With practice one can retire into this higher realm and look down, as it were with unconcern, upon the fever of life. In this upper stratum of consciousness one is entirely released from all worry, disappointment, grief and fear, or whatever it is that seeks to mar the life and disturb the mind. From this height one sees all the ambitions, greed and selfishness of the material life in their true perspective. One sees things in the light of eternity, one sees from the universal standpoint, and this cleanses the mind from every care and trouble and enables one to enter into perfect peace.

Anyone unpractised in this area who, after reading these words, tries to enter this higher mental realm, will find it impossible. This is due to lack of thought control and knowledge of how to use the mind. It is only through thought control and concentration that one can dismiss all worrying thoughts and enter the realm of perfect peace and calm.

It must be pointed out, however, that in addition to thought control, it is necessary to adjust the life into harmony with the laws which govern the universe. Students are shown how to free themselves of fear and adopt an attitude of mind towards life which is in harmony with the purpose of the divine scheme. When the right mental attitude is attained, and the student enters into harmony with the whole object and purpose of life; he enters into union with God; he thinks with God; he enters into the divine consciousness; he continually lives in the peace of the Infinite.

Chapter Twenty-Four

Self Development

The great object of this life is the development of character. This life is an opportunity given us to build up our character in certain directions. For instance, one person may have to overcome fear and worry, and develop trust. All the experiences of such a one's life will give him opportunities whereby he may fight this weakness. Another may have to overcome greed and selfishness, and he, too, will be given opportunities of fighting his failing, but whatever the weaknesses, it must be overcome. If we allow our life to slip by without overcoming our weaknesses, then we are in a bad way, for we shall have missed the very purpose of life. All true "thought" systems teach methods of overcoming weaknesses which, while not a royal road to quick and easy success, are a great help on the path.

There is no quick route.

One who has not discovered his inner spiritual powers tries to conquer by willpower alone. This is a joyless, painful and unprofitable method, and is extremely exhausting. The will should never be used in this way; instead, the inward spiritual power should be employed and directed by the divine Will. It is by this means alone that final victory can be achieved. All weaknesses and habits can be overcome by consciously using this inner power, but not without effort. It is a struggle between the higher self or lower self.

Self-control is possible only through thought control, for all action is the result of thought. One who cannot control his thoughts can never govern himself; he is literally a slave to his emotions and passions; he is a prey to every adverse condition which he meets. All habits can be mastered by using this technique. It is the same with every weakness of character; no matter what the weakness may be, it can be overcome by patient effort; by drawing upon the infinite power within; by thought control, and through directed constructive harmonious thinking. Lying dormant within each one of us is a spark of the divine perfection. The greatest object of this life is bringing the Divine into manifestation. We can do this only as we build up character, overcome habit and learn self-mastery, but not without effort.

Chapter Twenty-Five

Inspiration and Intuition

The ordinary mind of the senses learns from objective experiences, from the often-misleading evidence of the senses, from books, from the experience of others. It possesses no inspiration, no originality, no genius. All inspiration comes from within. Within each of us are divine powers lying dormant and unexpressed. Inspiration is one of them, and one who makes a daily practice of entering the "Secret Place of the Most High" experiences what is termed inspiration or direct knowing. One who receives inspiration in this way has received a call to service through inward inspiration. Emerson used to go into the woods and listen to the "voice of the woods". Great scientists and inventors have been "struck" by insight but, all of these ideas come from within, not from outside.

Within us also are powers of intuition or direct knowing which can be unfolded and used for our own guidance and the blessing of others. It takes time and needs patience to unfold these powers, but when it is accomplished, one is in touch with the deep wisdom of God.

Again, all originality comes from within. The surface mind can only copy the work of others and deduct by reasoning from known facts; true originality comes from the God within us. One who starts out on a fresh line of endeavour, or who brings a new idea to man, does so because he is divinely guided and instructed. We are each, if we could realise it, instruments through which the divine Mind brings light and guidance to men. By looking within to our divine centre, we learn to think constructively and creatively, we enter into fellowship with God, we become creators with Him.

One who learns to use his inner mind is greatly helped in the journey of life; he can, by relegating a problem to his inner mind, find a solution to every difficulty.

Chapter Twenty-Six

Success and Achievement

Success can only be won through spiritual power. He who cannot succeed shows that he has not learned to use his inner spiritual and mental powers. William Pollard, a Quaker and historian, writing on the spiritual basis of civilization, says:

"There is no opposition between the spiritual and the material ... far from there being any opposition, all material things good for man are discovered and made available by the use of his spiritual powers, and as long as he lives on this earth all his spiritual powers depend for their exercise on his body being supplied with air and food and drink ... economic advantages are a real asset which count for much; but they count for much very largely because they tend to fall into the hands of the spiritually vigorous races which have the energy and capacity to make the best of them ... there is more need at this day than in all our history for the secular spiritual gifts without which civilization cannot remain stable - for the powers of leadership, organisation, foresight, imagination, initiative, in all their degrees. The gifts are here. God has bestowed them abundantly on the human race ... there is a spiritual power which makes not only for success, but for righteousness, and which demands righteousness as the condition on which any lasting success is attained".

Success, then, depends upon spiritual power, and true lasting success can only be founded upon righteousness, justice, forgiveness and compassion to others. Every so-called success which is founded upon power, coercion, cruelty, exploitation and harshness to others has within it the seeds of its own decay.

Chapter Twenty-Seven

Good

To know and realise that through life and the universe runs the principle of infinite good is the first step towards happiness and success. To know that by consciously identifying oneself with the spirit of infinite good one can draw into one's life and body nothing but infinite good is to step out into a life of power and accomplishment.

God is infinite good; there is no evil in the divine scheme. When I look at a simple wayside flower, I realise in my soul that in beauty there is no evil; that there is only infinite good. Man possesses the divine power of thought. Thought is mind in motion; it is a spiritual power and is greater than any material power. Through the misuse of this power man turns the good forces of life into wrong channels and thus produces what we call evil.

War, addiction and cruelty towards others as well as self-inflicted are all the effect of wrong thinking. The power of evil is the collective effect of wrong thinking. If people could have right thought and cultivate love, then war, together with other disharmonies would end. Our divine Elder Brother taught us to think harmoniously and in love, but sadly, men have ignored His teaching. As a result, we have witnessed the strange anomaly of so-called Christian nations fighting one another with every imaginable cruelty. The power of providential energy can be directed by our thoughts into either good or negative courses; therefore, if we, by right thinking, direct it into the right channels, it manifests through harmony, peace, happiness, health and joy.

By wrong thinking man turns the good forces of life into disease, sickness, poverty and every kind of disharmony. But by thinking with God instead of against Him, we can manifest health, abundance and highest achievement; we can enter into peace, we can live a life of overcoming and indescribable joy.

Chapter Twenty-Eight

The Path of Attainment

The path of attainment is the way along which the soul passes in its climb from lower to higher things. It is not an easy path, because it does not follow that because one treads this path and makes the steep ascent to God, that one's outer life should be either poor or lacking in achievement. Indeed, the outward life should reflect the progress of the greater life within. The one should complement the other; for in the inner life, we learn the secrets of God's power, the strength, the perfection of His character, and in our outer life we should express these in the form of true success and achievement. The things which we achieve in life are not in themselves important, but the effect upon our character through the mastering of difficulties is of lasting benefit. For instance, to build up a big business is of no value in itself, for it brings added care and responsibility, and the things which can be bought with money quickly pall and cease to satisfy. But while achievement of this kind has no value in itself, its character-building effect is very valuable indeed. In the building up of a big business very high qualities are developed. One who builds up a huge business, and who keeps it, is tested and tried in every possible way. He has to exercise patience, courage, firmness, perseverance, faith, hope, self-control, vision and other qualities. The greater his difficulties, the more these qualities are developed. The business itself and the income that it brings are of little importance. Indeed, they are a great burden and responsibility and a comparatively poor man living a simpler life in a cottage is in all material respects better off; but the character-building effects are priceless. These qualities, won through ceaseless strife and overcoming, are added to the soul permanently. They remain with the soul all through the ages. They become part of the real spiritual man.

It will be seen then that in the outer world of achievement we are given an opportunity to manifest godlike powers to develop qualities of character through achievement and overcoming. It is not the path of everyone to become the architects of great businesses, neither are we all called to be great lawyers, politicians, writers or artists, but it is possible for each one of us to achieve success in the particular work which we have come here to do. Whatever our work in life may be, we have the ability, lying dormant within us, to achieve success in that work. In the doing of our work, in overcoming its difficulties, we build up character and qualities of mind and soul which are eternal and enduring in quality.

Even if we cannot achieve what the world calls success, we can enjoy the satisfaction of doing our work better than ever it has been done before, or as well as it is possible for it to be done, or for us to do it.

But it must be added, life is not what it seems to be. It is not governed solely by the harsh ways of men. Instead, it is controlled by spiritual laws and forces. It does not matter how shut in we may appear to be, nor how hopeless our outlook as regards promotion, advancement, improvement in circumstances or environment may also appear to be, there is nothing that can keep us from rising and advancing, and there is no one who can interrupt our progress but ourselves. The reason for this is that life is spiritual and is governed by inner laws. The Law is that as soon as we are ready for promotion we get it, and when we have outgrown one position in life, another and more advanced and responsible position opens up before us. The story of a person's advancement and achievement is the history of his mental expansion. As soon as he has assimilated one set of experiences and outgrown one position, other experiences and a higher position open before him. Therefore, if our future seems hopeless, it is only because we think it is so. All that we have to do really is to expand our mind, to push back its boundaries, and to think in larger ways. The same law applies to all walks of life and all modes of activity. The individual must first grow and expand in himself, before he can grow and expand in life's achievements. This growth and expansion has its origin in the thoughts. We must train our mind to think big thoughts and then to follow this up with hard work and the discipline that all progress demands.

Chapter Twenty-Nine

The Harmonious Life

The harmonious life is possible only to those who are harmonious thinkers. The outward life is a reflection of the greater life within. If our life is disharmonious, it is because of disharmonies within and it can only become harmonious when we inwardly adjust ourselves to the motive of life and the purpose of the divine scheme. All the disharmonies of life, its discords and irritations, have their cause within us and not outside us. The mind of the senses would have us look outside ourselves for the cause, but the inner teaching tells us to look within. The average person lays the blame on life, fate, other people or God, and often becomes very bitter about it. The longer we look outside us for the cause, and the more we lay the blame upon others, the worse our troubles grow, and the more conflicting our life becomes. The cause of conflict is not in other people or in outward circumstances; it is not in fate, neither is it the vindictiveness of God.

It is, instead, lack of adjustment with the purpose of life; lack of unity with the cosmic whole; it is disharmony with divine Will and Purpose.

If we return to the divine Source and harmonise our inner life with its purpose running through the whole cosmic scheme, we live a life of harmony and peace. We literally live in God; think with God; work with God and become attuned to the divine harmony. Our life expresses peace and love and reflects the calm of the Infinite. The things which formerly frustrated our hearts no longer affect us. We live our life in a higher vibration. Full of love and sympathy, we help others and endeavour to lead them to higher things. By the harmony of our own life, we become a restful influence on the lives of others; we bring peace and hope to troubled lives.

Chapter Thirty

Divine Optimism

Pessimism is antagonistic to the divine Idea. God is an eternal optimist; infinitely successful in all His undertakings. He has no thoughts of failure or despair or doubt. God can never be anything other than an optimist, for He *knows* that *all is well*. In the same way, if we think with God we naturally come in harmony with His will and purpose. We enter into the divine consciousness knowing that all is well. If we can see that although on the surface things may appear to be a mess, yet all is well with God's beautiful universe, we can never be a pessimist.

A pessimist is one who sees only the dark side of things and not knowing that these are the transient shadows, and that above is the eternal and perfect reality, becomes plunged into despondency. The more he meditates upon evil the more he believes in it. The more he believes in it the more it grows.

Pessimism is a philosophy of despair. It undermines the health; it holds one back from success; it robs the life of all joy and brightness; it makes one a depressing influence upon others. A pessimist is an enemy to himself and a source of depression and discord to others.

If the divine object of life is to come into harmonious union with God, then all pessimism must be replaced by an optimistic attitude towards life, and by a confident habit of thinking. No one who is a pessimist can know God, neither can one who knows God be a pessimist. One who knows God cannot help being an optimist, for he *knows* that *all is well*.

A philosophy of truth induces optimism. It is founded on the firm belief that the Creator knows what He is doing with His universe and that, in an interior sense, all is good, and *all is well*. It believes that ultimately there is no power but God's power and that this is good. It asserts that man has only to come into harmony with the infinite Love and automatically, by the operation of changeless and infinitely just law, he will enter into peace, happiness, abundance and health; he will receive every good and perfect gift, not in some future time or place, but *here and now*.

Chapter Thirty-One

The Greatest Of These Is Love

Love is the key to every situation in life; and by love is meant that kindly feeling that desires only the good for those we love. To cultivate thoughts of love, goodwill, forgiveness, pity, compassion, not only blesses and helps others, but it also brings happiness and harmony into our own life. In the Sermon on the Mount, we are told to agree with our adversary, and to love our enemies, and to do good to those who ill-treat us. This commandment need not be a tedious restriction, but it is an open door through which we can pass into a richer and fuller life. If we follow this commandment or advice, our life becomes filled with blessing, and our difficulties are overcome in a wonderful way. If, when we meet difficult people, we train ourselves to think thoughts of good will about them, and want positive things for them, we find that the difficulty is overcome, and harmony reigns instead. If certain people annoy us, and we allow ourselves to be annoyed, and if we sit in judgement upon them and magnify their faults and failings, then the annoyance increases, so that not only is our own life spoiled but also, we make life more difficult for the one whom we think is the cause of the trouble. But if, instead of allowing ourselves to be annoyed, we envelop the people who "rub up the wrong way", with thoughts of goodwill and try to look at things from their point of view, appreciating difficulties and troubles, and trying to see the God within them endeavouring to find expression then the whole situation becomes healed, and we are no longer annoyed. Also, through so doing we help the one who would otherwise annoy us, and this, of course, is the greatest thing we can do in life; help and bless other people and enable them to unfold and reveal the hidden splendour.

Again, if the barking of a dog irritates us, then if we actively start loving the dog, and become sympathetic and compassionate, the barking will either stop or will no longer have the power to annoy us.

Yet, again, if street musicians or beggars annoy us, if we think lovingly of them, instead of resentfully, then they to cease to irritate us. Whatever the situation may be, and no matter how difficult, *love is the key*. Love, when applied in this way, heals every situation, smooths every difficulty, and brings about a divine adjustment. When Jesus said that we should love one another, He gave us the secret of how to make our life harmonious, beautiful and happy. Many people have tried to follow the teaching of Jesus, simply as a commandment. They have tried to follow it because they have felt they ought to try to follow it, as a duty, if they are to be good Christians, but they have never realised, perhaps, that the advice of Jesus is not a boring and meaningless commandment, but an *open sesame* to a life of joy, freedom, and grace that is indescribable. If they had known this, they might have been more successful; for it is always easier to do a thing when we know the meaning of it, and what it is for, and what it leads to.

Then, again, many of those who have tried to follow the teaching have found it very difficult because they have not realised or understood the power of thought, or the necessity for training the thoughts to think in right channels. They have said: "But how can I love my enemies? I don't like them and never shall like them, so how can I feel love towards them?" However, I must point out that it is not a case of liking our enemies; and also, it is not a matter of feelings of affection. Love of the kind meant, is goodwill, compassion, tolerance and gentleness, giving of one-self, and one's very best to others. "God so loved the world that He gave His only begotten son", is more understandable if we say: "God so pitied the world", or "God had such compassion for the world".

What I want to speak of in closing is how thought and thought control can be used by us to help us to love our enemies. Our natural feeling is to resent what our enemies do to us, and to think thoughts of antagonism, of self-justification and condemnation. Doing this increases the trouble and causes matters to go from bad to worse. Instead, we can say: "I will not think thoughts of resentment or condemnation at all, but only thoughts of goodwill, forgiveness and compassion, and I will also pray that you may be blessed in every possible way". Then we can express our thoughts in definite words, such as "So and so [mentioning the name of our enemy] I love you, I forgive you, even as God loves and forgives me. I pray that you may be blessed in every possible way, and that you may find God and be filled with unspeakable joy". When we start doing this we may feel very far from loving, but the spoken word, which is a formed thought, has power, and if we *persevere* day after day, we gradually become changed until we really can love our enemy, and pray for his welfare as earnestly as for that of our nearest and dearest. When this is accomplished, the whole situation is found to be healed.

Also by Henry Thomas Hamblin

Thank you for purchasing this book. If you have enjoyed reading it, please consider leaving a review. It takes just a moment, and helps small publishers like us boost the visibility of our books, so that other readers can find our titles. Thank you – your time is much appreciated.

You can scan this QR code by holding your phone's camera to the code. A prompt will appear, which will take you directly to the 'leave a review' page.

To review in the US, please scan this QR code.

To review in the UK, please scan this QR code.

To review in Canada, please scan this QR code.

To review in Australia, please scan this QR code.

Also by Henry Thomas Hamblin

The Stillness of the Infinite: 18 Meditations to Deepen Spiritual Awareness through the Progressive Reflective Meditation Method

The Power of Thought: How to unlock the power of your mind to create a life of health, success, and prosperity

Within You is the Power: The Inner Secrets to Health, Happiness, Success and Abundance

The Secrets of Your Divine Powers: Reconnect with your Spiritual Self to Overcome Obstacles, Heal your Life and Achieve True Success

The Spiritual Path to True Success: The Practical Mystic's Guide to Living Successfully

The Message of a Flower: The Divine Wisdom in Nature

The Worry Antidote: The Practical Mystic's Guide to Living Fearlessly

The titles below are available from our website: www.thehamblinvision.org.uk

The Way of the Practical Mystic

My Search for Truth

The Story of my Life

Life Without Strain

Divine Adjustment

The Open Door

Life of the Spirit

His Wisdom Guiding

The Hamblin Book of Daily Readings

God Our Centre and Source

God's Sustaining Grace

HENRY THOMAS HAMBLIN

www.ingramcontent.com/pod-product-compliance
Lightning Source LLC
Chambersburg PA
CBHW030336010526
44119CB00047B/511